Either Ore

B.R. Snow

ISBN-13: 978-1-942691-01-3

Website: http://www.brsnow.net/
Twitter: @BernSnow

Acknowledgements

First, I'd like to thank all of my fans and readers for their ongoing support and friendship. I truly appreciate and am truly grateful for each and every one of you. And I love hearing from you so please keep sending those emails, tweets, texts…It may take me a while, but I do my best to respond to all of them. The best ways to contact me are:

Website: http://www.brsnow.net/
Email: bernsnow@gmail.com
Twitter: @BernSnow

Second, I'd like to extend a special thanks to my editor, Michelle Browne, a woman of intelligence and insight who possesses a terrific eye for detail. Her ability to ask the right questions and provide answers, when necessary, has made *Either Ore* a better book. To those of you out there looking for a quality editor of substance, your search is over.

Website: http://magpieediting.com
Email: shellebrowne@gmail.com

Finally, I'd like to thank my wife, Laurie, for her constant love and support. You make my life more fulfilled and so much easier in so many ways.

To Jeff

Someone who makes your life better simply by being in it.

1

*C*asper had strolled out of the second floor master bathroom, drying his hands with a monogrammed towel, when he saw the guy for the first time. Only ten minutes earlier, Casper had been cursing his inability to decipher the wall safe. But this guy already had it open, making Casper feel like a fucking amateur.

Casper had needed a break when his stomach, always touchy during B&E's, began fighting back against the extra-spicy, mega bean burrito he'd scarfed down earlier in the car. His stomach now settled into a slow roil, Casper leaned against the door and studied the guy taking items from the safe and sliding them into a large cloth sack. Casper snapped on a fresh pair of work gloves, then reached into his jacket pocket.

Upon hearing the *snap*, the guy emptying the safe turned and the small flashlight in his left hand lit the gun extending from Casper's right. Casper's first impression was that he was impressed by how the guy managed to stay so cool. Here he was, caught red-handed with a Glock pointed at his chest from eight feet, and the fucking guy just smiled and tossed another piece of jewelry in the bag. The room was dark, but Casper had seen enough sparkling to know that whatever it was, it was made out of diamonds. The guy glanced down into the bag, then back at Casper. The smile never left his face.

"Find what you were looking for?"

The guy focused on the Glock, probably deciding at that exact moment if Casper was going to shoot him, he'd have already done it.

The guy flashed that smile again.

"I guess. I was hoping for a bit more cash since, every time I have to fence jewelry, I always end up getting screwed on the exchange. But, yeah, I can make this work."

"I'm impressed," Casper said, nodding at the safe. "How'd you get it open? I was starting to think I was going to have to blast my way in."

"I can open anything." He shrugged. "Don't know why. It's just always been that way. When I was a kid, the neighbors were always stopping by the house when they had a pickle jar or some shit they couldn't open." He nodded at Casper's hand. "Triumph brand, right?"

Casper, still impressed by how in control the guy was, nodded and said, "You know, it's funny. I'm holding a gun that can turn you into hamburger, but you want to talk about gloves."

"Hey, every two bit thug out there carries a gun, but only a total pro would understand the importance of good gloves. Those the Triumph Micros?"

"Yeah, only ones I use," Casper said, starting to warm up to the guy.

"Me too," he said. "The Micros are super thin. And all the neurosurgeons and cardiologists swear by them. I've worn condoms that weren't as sensitive as these things."

"I'll remember that the next time I want to practice safe wanking." Casper pointed the Glock at the bag. "You want to put that down on the table next to the bed?"

"Not really," he said. "Whatever happened to possession is nine tenths of the law?"

"Nothing. But you're *possessing* a bag." Casper waggled the gun. "I'm possessing this."

"Is that the Glock 19?"

"Yeah."

"Shit, man. I've got the same model, right here in my pocket." The guy patted the right side of his jacket.

Casper fully extended the arm holding the gun. "You think you can get it out before I blow a hole the size of that safe in your chest?"

"Hey, relax, will ya? Don't go losing your fucking mind. I was just trying to make a point."

"And what would that be?"

"The point is that we got stuff in common. Same gloves, a smart business decision on both our parts that can't be underestimated. Same gun, lightweight but powerful. And reliable. When you need it, you damn well want to be sure it's gonna do the trick, right? Same kind of shoes, ones that are both quiet *and* comfortable. Shit, we even picked the same house to rob. Shows we have good taste and a sense of style."

"So?"

"So the point is, maybe it's a sign."

"A sign."

"Yeah, a sign that maybe the two of us should be working together. At a minimum, we could probably get a discount on gloves. You know, buying in bulk and all."

Casper laughed. Definitely the coolest crook he'd ever met. Guy staring down the barrel of a Glock but still able to find the funny and improvise on the fly. Casper shook his head.

"Sorry, I work alone."

"I got a ton of ideas, man. Really good ideas, but I'd need a partner to make some of them work. What do they say? Many hands make light work, or some shit like that."

"No, you got it right. So why don't you just *hand* it over and I'll be on my way. But feel free to help yourself to what's in the fridge before you go. That way your night won't be a total loss."

"Real funny. It ain't fair. Wasn't for me, you'd still be scratching your balls, wondering how to open that safe without waking up the whole neighborhood. Aren't you the least bit interested in what I've got to say? Or learning about my skill set?"

"Actually, what I'm interested in is what's in that bag." Casper wagged the gun at the small table next to the bed."

The guy held one hand up as a sign for Casper not to shoot him and inched his way toward he table. He slowly emptied the bag and trained the flashlight on the contents. "Earrings, necklaces, couple of bracelets...all diamond. Six Rolexes; three men's, three women's, if you can believe that. All those watches, and these rich pricks are probably so out of touch they don't even know what month it is, much less the time. Couple bundles of cash, looks like twenty K each. Not bad for fifteen minutes work...would have been less than that, if you hadn't felt the need to threaten me with a gun and slow down my progress." He stopped and cocked his head. "What the hell was that?"

"I didn't hear anything."

"Car door. Two of them...but soft, like somebody didn't want anybody to hear them close."

The guy crossed to the window and peered out through the side of the curtain. "Damn." He stepped back from the window, the smile gone.

"What is it?" Casper said, approaching the window. "Cops?"

"Worse. Security company. At least cops will give you a chance to give yourself up. The rent-a-cops the security companies hire are so bored most of the time, they'll shoot you just for something to do." He peered back through the curtain. "Goddamn it."

"What?"

"They're coming up the driveway. Two of them. A silent alarm must have gone off."

"That's not possible," Casper said. "I turned the security system off before I came in."

"Yeah, me too," he said. He paused and stared at Casper. "Shit."

"You must have turned it back on."

"Son of a bitch. How the hell did I do that?"

"Nice going, Mr. I Can Open Anything."

"I can," he said. "But I have a problem with computer shit."

"Ya think?"

They heard the front door click open and muffled voices downstairs in the foyer.

The guy turned the flashlight off.

"Well, how do you want to play it?" Casper whispered.

"Well, I sure don't want to stick around here and shoot it out with a couple of nine dollar an hour cowboys. I guess we'll need to go out the window."

The guy snuck another peek through the curtain then slowly slid the window open. He stuck his head out and looked both ways along the edge of the roofline. "There's a small ledge I think we can get to. We can climb out and work our way over to the garage. We should be able to jump down from there."

Casper poked his head through the window and did a quick assessment. "Okay, let's do it." Casper put his gun back in his pocket and started to climb through the window. The guy grabbed his shoulder.

"Hang on. One more thing," he whispered.

"What's that?"

"The stuff. How we gonna divide it up?"

Casper glanced at the table, then back at the guy. "Focused little prick, aren't you?"

"Hey, man," he said. "I'm trying to make a living here. This is business, not personal." He crossed to the table and refilled the bag. "Tell you what…you take the forty thousand in cash, I'll take the jewelry. By the time I get it fenced, I'll be lucky if I get anywhere near forty for all of it."

"Bullshit," Casper whispered. "My three-year-old nephew could get forty for all that."

"Be that as it may," the guy said. "I'm still getting the short end of the stick, but it ain't like either one of us is in much of a position to stand here and haggle."

Casper thought for a moment, then nodded and stuffed the two bundles of cash into his pocket. "Okay, let's go."

The guy folded the bag and placed it inside his jacket, then zipped it tight. He watched Casper swing his legs out the window, then heard a soft thud as he landed on the ledge below. He looked down. Casper, through the moonlight, gave him a thumbs up. He swung his legs out the window and joined Casper on the ledge. Facing the house, they inched along the ledge shuffling sideways.

"By the way," Casper said. "I'm Casper Dupree."

"Good to meet you. I'm Either Ore."

"Either or what?"

"Either or fucking nothing. That's my name."

Casper continued to shuffle along the ledge heading towards the garage roof. "Either? Your name is Either?"

"Yeah. Either Ore. That's O.R.E. You got a problem with that, *Casper*?"

"No. No problem. Your parents must have a sense of humor."

"They liked to think so."

"Pretty unusual. Be a hard name to forget," Casper said, slowing a bit as they approached the garage.

"Yeah, well, if you end up getting pulled in by the cops, just make sure it manages to slip your mind."

"No problem. I've never divulged anything to the cops in my life, and I'm not about to start. And I'm safe assuming you'll extend me the same courtesy?"

"Man, do you ever listen to yourself? Sometimes you sound like you're trying to come across as some kind of professor."

"Fine. How's this…can you keep your fucking mouth shut if you get arrested?"

"No worries there. I already forgot your name, *Casper*."

They reached the point where the ledge met the garage roof, jumped, and each landed with a soft thud. They walked to the edge of the garage roof and looked down.

"It's only about ten feet," Casper said, staring down at the concrete driveway. "If we tuck and roll, we shouldn't break anything."

"That's very comforting," Either said, looking down for a landing spot.

Casper checked that the two bundles of cash were secure, then inched his way to the edge of the garage room. "See you on the other side."

Either came to a stop.

"Wait, I heard something."

"Man, you got good ears," Casper said. "What is it?"

"Sounded like a growl."

Casper peered down through the darkness.

"Shit, you're right. Dog."

"Dog? Fuck."

"Big dog…cop dog."

"Rottweiler?"

"No. German Shepherd. Where'd you ever see a Rottweiler that was a cop dog?"

"I'm telling you, I've seen it." Either started walking in small circles. "Damn. I hate dogs. Especially cop dogs."

"How can anybody hate dogs? What the hell is the matter with you?"

"Let's just say I'm scared of them and leave it at that."

"Well, suck it up," Casper said. "Let's go."

"Not with that dog down there."

"You'd rather stay here and get shot?"

"Hey, I raise my arms up here, I don't get shot. I raise my arms down there, the only thing I do is make it easier for that dog to bite my balls off."

Casper glanced back towards the house. Lights were coming on one room at a time as the security guards conducted their search. Casper reached down and removed his shoes. He whistled softly, then threw one into a large shrub off to one side of the garage. He heard a growl and the sound of the dog's nails scratching on the concrete. Silence. Then they both heard a throaty growl directly underneath them on the ground below.

"Jesus Christ," Casper said. "Listen to that."

"I'm trying not to," Either said.

Casper threw his second shoe deeper into the shrub. The dog barked and scrambled off towards the bush.

"Okay, it's now or never," Casper said.

Either, paralyzed with fear, shook his head. "Never."

"You're joking, right? You'd rather get arrested than take your chances with a dog?"

"You ever see how much damage a pissed off cop dog can do?"

"Okay, it's your funeral." Casper jumped off the garage, landed and tumbled, managing to only bang his knee and roll an ankle. He scrambled to his feet and looked up. "You coming or not?"

"Where's the dog?" Either said.

"He's in the bushes, but I'm sure he'll be back soon. C'mon."

"No. I can't do it."

"Don't be such a pussy," Casper said, shaking his head.

Either stayed right where he was.

"Well, at least toss down the bag."

"Are you out of your fucking mind?"

"You want to give it back? Or get arrested holding it?"

"Shit." Either unzipped his jacket and tossed the bag down to Casper, who caught it, then started running up the driveway with a limping gait.

"And I want it back. You hear me?"

Either's voice, well above a whisper, caught the dog's attention. It returned to the driveway and sat growling directly below the fear-stricken Either. Casper paused halfway up the driveway and watched the two security guards climb out a bedroom window onto the garage roof.

"Freeze, asshole!"

8

Either slowly raised his hands and turned to face them as they slowly worked their way across the roof.

"Don't fucking move!"

"Relax cowboy," Casper heard Either say. "I know the drill."

2

*T*he second time Casper saw Either was when a tattooed hand tossed a copy of *Love Blooms Slowly* on the table in front of him.

"Just make it out to 'my tight-lipped friend, Either.'"

Casper studied the tattoo; it was low quality and looked like some kind of bird, possibly a chicken. He placed his Sharpie on the table, removed his glasses, and looked up.

"How you doing, Either?"

"Tortoise-shell?" Either said, nodding at Casper's glasses. "Man, you got all the bases covered, don't you?"

"Last time I saw you, you were cowering on top of a garage," Casper said. He picked up his glasses and began wiping the lens with a tissue. "How long has it been?"

Either's eyes scanned the bookstore, then refocused on Casper. "I wasn't cowering." Either stared into a distant corner of the store. "Damn dog."

"Yeah. He was a real bruiser. He almost got me but I managed to-"

"We need to chat," Either said. "After you sign my book. Twenty-four bucks. For that much money, you should fucking read it to me." Either picked it up, studied the inscription, then closed the book and stood waiting. "You ready?"

Casper nodded and stood. "Yeah, sure. The crowd's pretty light at the moment, and I'm about due for a break."

"At the moment?" Either said, laughing. "Man, I've been here almost an hour, and you sold what, five, maybe six books? Hope I don't get crushed when all your fans rush the stage." Either laughed louder.

"I sold seven," Casper waved to one of the bookstore employees. "Sally, I'm going to take a break. I'll be back in fifteen." He turned to Either. "You want coffee? They got a Starbucks here."

"Starbucks in a bookstore. Is this a great country or what? No, after thirty-seven months inside, I'm thinking something a bit stronger. Let's wander across the street."

"Sure. Whatever you say. I'm buying."

"Damn straight you're buying."

Either led the way across the street to a small neighborhood bar. Inside, it was dark, rank and empty. A lone bartender was building a tower out of swizzle sticks and filling an ashtray with butts.

Casper removed his jacket and draped it over the back of the booth. He slid into his seat and scanned the bar.

"This place is barely hanging on against the incessant encroachment of fast-food franchises and the mini-mall."

"You gonna keep talking like that, Professor, or am I going to have to slap the shit out of you?"

Casper shook his head then held up his hands in surrender. He took another quick look around the bar. "Okay…this place is a fucking dump. You happy?"

"Hey, I'm back out in the free world. I'm delighted. Give me a twenty. I'll get the drinks. What do you want?"

Casper tossed a twenty on the table. "A shot of Jack and a beer."

"How about that? I thought for sure you'd be a wine spritzer kinda guy."

"Just get the drinks so we can get on with this."

Either snatched the twenty off the table and headed to the bar. Casper glanced around the bar then watched Either return to the table, carrying a tray. He set the drinks on the table and tossed the tray into the booth behind him.

Casper waited, but finally asked. "Where's my change?"

Either tossed back a shot and wiped his mouth with the back of his hand. "Change? There's no change. I have a reputation as a good tipper I need to maintain."

"I see," Casper said, tossing back his shot of Jack Daniels.

"Besides, he was running low on cigarettes and swizzle sticks. Poor bastard." Either leaned forward and nodded in the general direction of the bartender. "You know what he is, Professor?"

Casper glanced at the bartender, then shrugged and said, "Apart from his obvious role as a mixologist, I wouldn't have a clue."

"Well, you should…you being a writer and all. Aren't you supposed to be observant? Able to make observations about your fellow man?"

"I guess," Casper said, taking a sip of beer.

Either continued to stare hard at Casper. "What that bartender is, Professor…is a cautionary tale."

"Is he now?"

"You think when he was just a little boy he dreamed of growing up to become a bartender in a shithole like this? 'You wanna be a baseball player, Timmy?' 'Nah.' 'Okay, how about a musician, or maybe a famous scientist?' 'No, Dad, I want to grow up and try to exist on tips from alcoholics who can't even afford the cost of their next drink.'"

"Vivid," Casper said, nodding. "Not bad."

"I have my moments," Either said, starting to work on his beer. "Cautionary tales, Professor. And if you don't make smart choices these days, this country will run you over and turn you into a cautionary tale faster than you can overuse a metaphor."

"This is all very interesting, Either. But is there a point to this conversation?"

"Of course there's a point. You think I'd spend all this time tracking you down and agreeing to come into this shithole if I didn't have a point?"

"Well, good. I'd love to hear it." Casper finished his beer and slid the bottle away.

"The point, Professor, is that there are millions of cautionary tales in this country. I just spent three years surrounded by them. That shouldn't come as a surprise to anyone. You go to prison, you expect the place to be filled with

12

people you should do the exact opposite of what they've spent their lives doing."

"Kind of an odd sentence structure, but, yeah, I get your point."

Either waved a hand at the bartender, then continued. "But what is really interesting, to me anyway, is that now I'm out and back on the streets, I see them everywhere. I guess they've always been around, but I guess I never really paid attention. They're everywhere. The bored, the scared, the lifeless…the indifferent, the mean and nasty, you name it. And they all have something in common. You know what that is, Professor?"

"I really wouldn't have a clue."

"And you call yourself a writer."

After managing to sell a mere seven books in the past three hours, Casper was beginning to wonder how much longer he could continue to call himself that. He sat back as the bartender approached carrying a fresh tray of drinks.

Either flashed that smile at the bartender as he unloaded the drinks. "Perfect timing, my man. Thanks." He looked across the table at Casper. "Give the man a twenty."

Casper handed over another twenty, caught Either's glare, and told the bartender to keep the change.

"Well done, Professor. It's good for your Karma."

"I could use it," Casper said, tossing back his shot.

"Man, can't we all." He took a gulp of beer, tossed his own shot, gulped again. He sighed contentedly and leaned back with his arms draped across the booth. He nodded in the direction of the bartender. "Never underestimate the power of good tipping."

"I'll remember that."

"You see, Professor. Most people would come in here, take one look at that guy and put him in the box marked loser. Maybe even give him a rash of shit just to fuck with him. You know, one cautionary tale's gift to another. And then the bartender would get right back at him with his own brand of

13

shit. You know I'm right. But not me. I treat him as the hard working equal he is."

"You're a saint, Either. What can I say?"

"Well, thank you, Professor. Which brings me to my point about cautionary tales."

Casper took a long pull from his beer, then glanced down at his watch.

"Relax, Professor. If you've got a couple of horny housewives who get wet reading your books and took the time to drive all the way out here just to get your autograph, they'll wait until you get back."

"I'm fine. Don't worry about it."

"Do I look worried?" Either leaned forward with both elbows on the table. "You see, Professor, the thing that all cautionary tales have in common is that they always let everybody else know they're a cautionary tale."

Casper shook his head. "That's some sage wisdom you got there, Grasshopper. Real enlightening. You become a Buddhist in prison, Either?"

Either drained his beer and waved at the bartender. "Not a chance. Man, you get three people together in prison and the next thing you know they're joining one religion or another. The Buddhists were pretty cool but they're so passive and few in numbers they were always getting the shit beat out of them. The Catholics just tried to make me feel guilty. And the damn Born Agains were always…what's the word I'm looking for?"

"Proselytizing?"

"Yeah, that's it. Those freaks were always trying to convert me. 'Repent sinner. Convert now, before Jesus returns. Save your soul while there's still time.' You ask me, Jesus ain't coming back until he's convinced he ain't gonna have to deal with those fuckers when he gets here."

Casper laughed and shook his head.

"There you go, Professor. Finally, you're relaxing. Now reach into that pocket and give our man Jimmy another twenty."

Either glanced up at the bartender who was already standing next to the table with a fresh tray of drinks and smiled. Either waited until he departed, twenty dollar bill in hand, then continued.

"And don't even get me started on the Muslims. I know there's a whole bunch of cool Muslims out here in the real world. But the ones they got locked up are some scary motherfuckers. Man, talk about your collection of cautionary tales. You join that group in lockup, you better have a high tolerance for prayer and impromptu bomb building." Either gazed off into the distance then looked back at Casper. "But, yeah, the Buddhists were pretty cool. Cautionary tales, but did a pretty good job of not showing it."

Casper glanced at his watch again then shrugged and downed his shot. Either leaned back in the booth, relaxed, a couple of drinks down, a fresh one on the table in front of him. Casper watched him. It's coming soon he decided. Whatever Either had in mind, it wouldn't be long now before he laid it out. He waited and then Either flashed that smile.

"You want to hear something funny?"

"Sure," Casper said. "I'm always up for a good laugh."

"Well, I'm not sure if you're actually gonna laugh. I mean it's funny, but not necessarily ha-ha funny. It's...what's the word I'm looking for?"

"I wouldn't have a clue."

"You know, Professor, you're the writer, but I'm the one doing all the work. What's the word for when something happens that is pretty much the opposite of what you might expect and it leaves you scratching your head or laughing?

"Ironic."

Either raised his shot glass in toast. "There you go, Professor. Ironic. Cool."

"Glad I could help move the story along."

Either turned serious and leaned forward again. "It was the weirdest thing I saw the whole time I was in. I come into the rec room after dinner one night - they call it a rec room, but this bar

15

would be an improvement over that thing. There's only one other guy in there, stretched out on the couch. So I'm minding my own business and I turn on the TV…some piece of shit model that must have been twenty years old bolted onto the wall. Damn remote didn't even work…can you imagine that? Having to manually change the channel?"

"The horror."

"Exactly. Anyway, I was getting ready to watch my show."

"Let me guess. You're an Oprah fan."

"The hell with that. Don't get me wrong. I got tons of respect for her as a businesswoman, but I can't watch that shit. Nah, I watch *House Hunters*. Especially the international one. I watch that show and think about how easy it would be to do B&Es in most of those places. All the rich Yanks and Euros kicking back near the beach with their windows open to let the sea breezes in. Just walk right in, then walk right out. Piece of cake."

"Well, I guess it's good to have a dream."

"Exactly. So anyway, I turn the volume up so I can hear the names of the towns where these people are buying…you know, just in case."

"Sure. You might as well get some good background information if they're just giving it away."

"You got that right. So I'm minding my own business when the guy on the couch tells me the TV is bothering him and to turn the fucking thing off. Not down, mind you, off."

"The nerve of some people."

"So I turn around, and guess what he was doing."

"I can't imagine."

"Well, try to imagine, Professor. Isn't that your job?"

Casper shook his head then spread his hands open. "He was trying to take a nap."

"Wrong. He was bawling his eyes out."

"Had you turned him down in the shower?"

"Yeah, I had. But that had been a couple of months earlier. I stuffed a bar of soap down his throat, so by that time, we had

16

pretty much come to an understanding about that shit." Either placed both elbows on the table and stared at Casper. "He was reading."

"Reading?"

"A book. And not just any book. One of yours."

"Really?" Casper pondered the idea of a convict weeping over his writing. "How about that?"

"That's what I thought too. Big black guy. About six-five, close to three bills, doing twenty years for a double manslaughter that was pled down because they couldn't find the murder weapon that, by the way, just happened to be stuffed inside a victim's head."

"Couldn't they get it out of the head?"

"Well, I'm sure they could have if they had ever found it."

"Ugh. Jesus."

"Yeah. You look up the definition of cautionary tale in the dictionary and you'll see this guy's picture. But the point is, Professor, here's this guy, who'd just as soon shoot you as look at you, bawling his eyes out because some housewife piece of trim got her heart broke by some scum-bag life insurance salesman."

"*Term of Life.*"

"So I just had to see what sort of book could make a guy like that turn on the waterworks."

"It's a tragic story. You see when Gwendolyn-"

Either stopped him with a raised palm.

"Never mind," Casper said. "It's not important."

"The guy hands me the book and I'm looking at it, you know, wondering what the hell is going on. Then I turn it over. Guess what I saw?"

"My photo on the back cover?"

"Now you're cooking, Professor. At first I couldn't place you. I knew I'd seen you someplace before. Then your name clicked." Either drained his beer. "Now why didn't you tell me you were a writer when we met?"

"I guess because we were busy doing other things. Besides, I was writing back then, but I hadn't been published."

"And now you are."

"I self-publish as an independent. I'm what they call an indie."

"So you ain't got a publisher or an agent bossing you around or looking over your shoulder?"

"No. It's just me."

"That's even better."

"Better? For who?"

"For us, my friend."

"Either, you lost me."

"Patience, my man. Just be patient. What's your schedule like?"

"My schedule?"

"Yeah, how many events like the one across the street...what do you call them?"

"Signings."

"Signings," Either said, committing it to memory. "How many signings you got coming up over the next couple of months?"

"None. I'm just doing this one as a favor to Sally."

"The cute little blonde?"

"Yeah. She owns the bookstore."

"She get wet reading your books?"

"Wet?"

"Yeah, wet. Moist between the thighs. A little hot dampness to go with all those salty tears."

"I wouldn't have a clue."

"Bullshit. You've been doing her for a while now. I knew it as soon as I walked in."

"You're quite the detective," Casper said. He glanced at his watch. If he didn't get back soon, he wouldn't be doing her tonight. Sally didn't like promises broken and wasn't shy about showing it.

"You know, I read one of your books."

"Really?"

"Yeah, I figured since we were going to be working together, I should at least be familiar with your work."

"Working together? What are you talking about?"

"All in good time, Professor." He stood up and arched his back. "C'mon. We need to get you back before Blondie starts to dry out."

Casper climbed out of the booth and followed Either to the door.

"So what did you think?" Casper said.

"About what? Your writing?"

"Yeah."

"It was okay. Not really my thing, but you do know how to tell a story. Gotta give you that. But you need to come up with another description for the old one-eye trouser snake. If I had to read one more time about his *throbbing manhood*, I was gonna puke."

"It's a metaphor. That's a-"

"I know what a fucking metaphor is. Just call it what it is. I'm sure your readers can handle it."

"I'll think about it." Casper tugged at his jacket and smoothed the sleeves. He shot his cuffs and stepped outside. "Anything else I should work on?"

"Yeah. Start looking for bookstores located in mini-malls on the Northwest coast."

"Why would I do that?"

"Because I've never been up there, that's why."

"No, I meant why should I start looking for bookstores located in mini-malls?"

"Because, Professor, you and I are about to embark on an extended book tour."

"Embark?"

"Good word, huh? Kind of makes my manhood throb."

"After three years in the joint, I would think that '*Whassup?*' would be enough to do the trick."

"Man, you got that right."

3

*W*hen the doorbell rang, Casper, annoyed by the interruption, crossed to the door and pulled it open. Either stood waiting, arms loaded, impatiently nodding his head. Casper stepped back as Either staggered towards the dining room table. He dropped a collection of folders and a couple of long cylindrical cardboard tubes on the table, then handed Casper a case of beer. Either held onto the bottle of Jack Daniels. He nodded at the case of beer.

"That needs to go in the fridge," Either said, "And we'll need a couple of glasses with ice."

"Well, just come on in and make yourself at home," Casper said.

Either stood next to the table, organizing the folders. "I thought later we'd just order pizza." He paused to think for a moment. "Or maybe Chinese."

Casper stared at Either, then adjusted the case of beer under his arm and went to the kitchen. Either sat and refocused on the folders. Casper returned with the glasses, poured both then sat down across from Either.

"What's in the folders?"

Either lit a cigarette and emptied a couple of the folders on the table. "Photos, background information. Just some basic research to get us started."

"I thought I told you I wasn't interested in whatever wild-ass scheme you've dreamed up."

Either took a drag from his cigarette, then placed it in an ashtray. "You did." He flashed Caper that smile.

"Then it should be pretty clear," Casper said. "I'm out of that business. Understand?"

"Sure, Professor." Either picked up a document and began flipping through the pages. "Just hand me a bag with…oh, let's say a hundred grand, and I'll be on my way."

"A hundred grand? Why the hell would I do that?"

"You owe me."

"For what?"

"For getting the total proceeds from our last job," Either said, refilling his glass. "Thought I forgot about that, huh?"

Casper started to respond but stopped.

"And let's not forget my ability to keep my mouth shut and take the bullet for both of us. I probably could have pled it down if I'd been willing to give you up, but I didn't. Did I?"

"No."

"Exactly. Lucky for you I consider myself an old-school kind of guy."

"But I don't have a hundred grand to give you."

"We could probably debate that all day, but let's not," Either said, flashing that smile Casper no longer found cool. Either spread his arms open, glanced down at the table, then back up at Casper. If anything, the grin had widened. "Thereby…I thusly reveal to you…the plan." The smile disappeared and he shook his head. "Man, I don't know how you can talk shit like that and still live with yourself, Professor."

"What can I say? A good vocabulary is a real burden to walk around with."

"Yeah, I'm sure. Now shut the fuck up and pay attention."

Casper stood and looked in the hallway mirror, patting a stray hair back in place.

"Look, maybe we can do this another time. I really need to get back to my writing."

Either scoffed and lit a fresh cigarette.

"No, really," Casper said. "This is one of my writing days."

"Sit."

"You're putting me off my schedule."

"You don't sit down I'm going to be putting you out that window."

"But-"

"Your schedule is just going to have to wait." Either glared at him. "End of discussion. Sit. And stay there."

"Maybe you should revisit your phobia. You'd be good with dogs."

"Yeah, like that's gonna happen." Either focused on the documents in front of him on the table. "This one, I have to say, is truly genius. It's so good that we'd be put in the criminal hall of fame, first ballot." Either paused to drink. "They'd probably even waive the waiting period."

Casper topped off both glasses as he watched Either get organized.

"Have you always spent your time dreaming up wild-ass schemes or is this something new you picked up in the joint?"

Either considered the question. "I've always been creative I guess. Just like you."

Casper laughed. "Just like me, huh?"

"Yeah, just like you. I spend a lot of time thinking up all sorts of goofy shit. The difference is I don't waste my time writing it all down."

"So you're saying my writing is a total waste of time?"

"Don't get your knickers in a knot, Professor."

"No," Casper said. "I'd like to know."

"Know what? Whether those panty moisteners you write are a waste of time?"

"Yeah."

"How would I know? I don't wear 'em."

"You seem to have an opinion about everything else. C'mon. Tell me."

Either crushed his cigarette out. "Let's just say they're a means to an end and leave it at that."

Casper, holding his drink across his chest with both hands, sat back in his chair and pouted. Either picked up a photo and tossed it across the table.

"Lighten up. I'd like you to meet Mr. Jack Whitehead."

Casper turned the photo around and studied the smiling man standing in front of a building draped with banners. "The name sounds familiar."

"It oughta," Either said tapping the photo with his finger. "He's the McDonald's of mini-malls."

"I beg your pardon?"

"I don't know what about that sentence could be con…what's the word I'm looking for?"

"Construed?"

"Yeah. Construed. What about that sentence could be *construed* as confusing?"

"I didn't get the McDonald's reference, that's all."

"You ever drive around and see one of those mini-malls with the red tile roofs?"

"Sure. They're all over the place."

"Always find them in nice neighborhoods with a lot of the same high-end stores."

Casper helped himself to one of Either's cigarettes, took a drag and exhaled up at the ceiling. "Now that you mention it, I think you're right."

"Of course I'm right. You think I'm just making this shit up?"

Casper sighed. "Please continue."

"Guess how many of these cookie-cutter monstrosities Mr. Whitehead, our boy Jack, has built."

"I have no idea."

"Did I ask you to tell me how many he's built? I said guess."

"Jesus, you're in a mood." Casper thought for a moment. "A hundred?"

"Four hundred and seventy-six. In twenty-seven states."

"Wow. That's a lot." Casper straightened up in his chair. "Now I remember him. 60 Minutes or somebody like that did a feature on him a couple years ago."

"Exactly. I saw that story in the joint, and it was like Christmas had come early." Either refilled both glasses and leaned forward, his voice falling to a whisper. "If you live in an upscale zip code, there's a good chance he's built one of these things in your neighborhood."

"So he's not really McDonald's then," Casper said.

Either frowned and sat back. "What are you talking about?"

"Well, McDonald's are considered more of a middleclass establishment."

"You saying rich people don't eat at McDonald's?"

"No. That's not what I'm saying. I just think your analogy could be strengthened."

"Enough." Either crushed out his cigarette. "Okay, so he's the fucking Red Lobster of mini-malls. Happy?"

"Well, actually-" Casper caught Either's glare and nodded. "Rhetorical question. Got it. Sure. Red Lobster it is."

"Moving on." Either flashed the smile. "What's one thing you notice when you see one of them in those nice neighborhoods?"

"What?"

"Man, it's a simple question. Are you dense or just screwing with me?"

"You asked me to identify one thing. But I notice a lot of different things about the country these days. If you read my books, you'll see that I weave a lot of my social observations into my writing."

"Yeah, right between the episodic throbbing of your manhood."

"I told you before. It's a metaphor."

"Relax, Professor. Let me be more specific. When you see one of those red-tile jobbies, what's your first thought?"

Casper stood up and stared down at the photo. "Well, let's see. One thing is they're very recognizable."

"Exactly. They're upscale, but still cookie cutter. If you find something that works, people tend to stick with it. Our boy Jack calls it part of his…"

"Branding strategy," Casper said.

"Yeah, that's it." Either opened one of the tubes and extracted the contents.

Casper leaned forward.

"What's that?"

Either unrolled the large sheets of paper.

"The master plan, man. Blueprints. This is Whitehead's master plan."

"Where did you get your hands on them?"

"I know a guy who's a hacker and just got out of a minimum security joint in California. He got them right off Whitehead's computer system somehow. Like I said when we first met, apart from cracking safes, I ain't very good with technology."

Casper studied the plans. "Impressive."

"Yeah. And it only cost you five grand."

"Me?"

"Relax, Professor. In a few weeks, that will be pocket change. You can pay me back later. Oh, and remind me at some point that we need to send him a nice pair of diamond earrings. He went up for eighteen months and his wife's still pretty pissed. He's got an anniversary coming, and he thinks something sparkly might help."

Casper sat back in his chair and rubbed his chin.

"What's the matter?" Either said, looking through the stack of documents.

"That's only one set of plans," Casper said. "You said the guy has built close to five hundred of these things."

"I already told you they're cookie cutter."

"Yeah, but they can't all be the same...nobody would be dumb enough to...would he?"

Either beamed at him and handed him a document. "Take a look."

Casper began flipping through the pages. "What's this?"

"It's the transcript of an interview Whitehead did a couple of years ago with some building trade magazine. The dumb bastard must have been drinking when he did it."

As Casper read, Either refilled both glasses and lit a cigarette. He sat waiting with a huge smile.

"Holy shit," Casper said.

"Yeah, he just lays it all out there, doesn't he? How the secret to his competitive advantage is to *replicate* everything right down to the number of steel beams and bolts he uses. Buys in bulk to keep his costs low and uses the same companies for...what's he call them?"

Casper scanned the document until he found the reference. "Associated ancillary systems."

"Yeah, that's it. The guy just has to have a million-dollar-word for it."

"Phrase."

"What?"

"It's actually a phrase, not a word."

Either glared at him until Casper picked up his drink, breaking eye contact.

"Never mind," Casper said. "Not important."

"Thank you. Guess what one of those ancillary systems is?"

"The security system."

"Now you're cooking, Professor."

Casper continued to flip through the pages. "Don't tell me he mentions the company he partners with."

"I tell you, the dumb bastard must have been hammered. I can just see him sitting there like a peacock, laying it all out."

Casper landed on the page he was looking for, read for a moment, then glanced up. "Son of a bitch. Oxkeyless Systems." He tossed the document on the table. "They're okay. But I've cracked a bunch of them over the years."

Either smiled, picked up the bottle of Jack Daniels, and poured. "I was so hoping you'd say that."

"Okay," Casper said. "This is good information but-"

"Good? It's gold."

"Yes, I can see that. But how do you plan on using it?"

"Let me ask you a question, Professor."

"Here we go again."

"In those cookie cutter malls, guess how many have bookstores? And if you say you don't have a clue, I'll whack you in the head with that bottle of Jack."

Casper sighed. "Okay, let's see. Almost five hundred. I'll say five percent of them have a bookstore. That's my guess." He glanced at Either. "That would be twenty-five."

"I can do the math, Professor. No, you're not even close. Eighty one."

"Wow I'm surprised. With what's going on in the book business these days, I didn't think there'd be that many."

"Yeah. But we better hurry. They're closing fast."

"I'm still not seeing any plan here."

"Of course you don't. I haven't revealed it yet."

It was Casper's turn to glare. "I'm so glad to hear that. I would hate for you to think I was obtuse."

Either shrugged and took a drag on his cigarette.

"I wouldn't call you that, Professor. Dumb as a post sometimes, but not obtuse. You look like you keep yourself in pretty good shape. Okay, next question. What other kind of store might you expect to find in one of these red-tiled shopping traps?"

"Hey, that's not bad." Casper closed his eyes. "I'm getting an image akin to a spider web. A spider web of crass consumerism."

"Good for you. Feel free to steal it. Answer the question."

"Let's see. Well, you got high-end clothing stores, kitchen gadgets, electronics, Victoria's Secret or something similar and...son of a bitch...jewelry stores."

Casper's smile matched Either's for the first time. Either headed to the kitchen and returned with two beers. He handed one to Casper and hovered at the edge of the table.

"You know what I'm going to ask you, don't you?"

"You want me to guess how many jewelry stores are located in the eighty-one with bookstores."

"Now you're on your game, Professor."

Casper thought, drumming the tabletop with one hand. "I'm going to go low and say…there's nine jewelry stores."

"Thirty-four."

"Unbelievable." Casper stood and started pacing. "This could work."

"Could? Professor, with your ability to disable security systems and my skills cracking safes, there's no doubt it's gonna work."

"Sure beats trying to make a living selling books. This could be big."

"It's huge. It's the ultimate retirement plan."

"But how do we do it so they don't make the connection?"

"What connection? You're just there to do a book signing. And I'm your business manager. If some jewelry stores can't protect themselves from a couple of creative types like you and me, I tell you, Professor, it ain't our problem. And these stores are all over the country. Different bookstore owners. Different jewelry stores. There's no logical pattern. Nothing to link them, apart from the fact that the mini-malls were all built by the same guy. And who'd ever be smart enough to figure that one out? Besides, if somebody did ever manage to put it all together, we'll be long gone down the road."

"You lost me."

"Who's dense now?"

"No, I think I have some idea about what you're talking about. But how do we manage to keep a low profile?" Casper said, sitting back down.

"Why the fuck would we do that? Low profile is the opposite of what we're going for. We're gonna tell the whole world we're there."

"We are? Why?"

"Because the last person they'd expect is someone who makes a huge entrance and does everything he can to draw

28

attention to himself. Plus, it would be nice to sell some books, right?"

"I…yeah, I guess." Casper, lost, looked across the table. "Either, I'm sorry but I don't have a clue what you're talking about."

Either stood and jingled a set of car keys in front of Casper. "I've saved the best for last. Follow me." He headed towards the door. Casper finished his beer, then followed Either outside. When he reached the curb, his mouth dropped.

"Not bad, huh?"

"What is it?"

"What do you think it is? It's a Winnebago. Our new home for the next few months. You like it?"

Casper scanned the custom paint job. His book jacket photo dominated the front portion of the vehicle. In big letters that ran along the side he saw 'Casper Dupree's Endless Book Tour' in an elaborate font. Underneath that, the covers of his book were on display. Stunned, he looked at Either.

"The paint job cost you a fortune," Either said. "Twenty grand, but you can pay me back later." He gently rubbed a hand across one of Casper's book covers as he admired the outside of the massive vehicle. "The rental's ten grand a month, but you'll be able to handle it. Worth every penny."

Either watched Casper continue to stare at the Winnebago.

"Well look at that. The Professor is speechless. Miracles do happen."

4

*E*ither squeezed the leather-wrapped steering wheel and beamed. Cocooned behind his Oakley Oil Rig wraparounds, he focused on the long stretch of highway ahead of them and checked their speed. He stretched his legs, exhaled loudly and glanced at Casper sitting in the plush pilot's seat to his right.

"Man, just look at that."

Casper looked up from the laptop in his lap, glanced at Either, then at the road outside. He looked back at Either. "What am I supposed to be looking at?"

"Sixty-eight."

"Sixty-eight? It's the desert out there. It's gotta be at least in the nineties."

"I'm not talking about the goddamn temperature."

"Too bad," Casper said, pulling on a sweatshirt. "It's freezing in here."

"Jesus Christ," Either said, shaking his head.

"Well, what are you talking about?"

"Never mind." Either tightened his grip on the steering wheel and wiggled his bare toes. "What a fuckwit."

"Okay," Casper. "I'll play. Let's see. Sixty-eight. That's where your girlfriend asks for a sixty-nine and you tell her to go ahead and get started, but you'll have to owe her one."

"Wrong," Either said. He glanced at Casper. "Is that really what that's called?"

"Dumbass." Casper resumed typing.

"Cruise control," Either said, nodding at the speedometer. "I was referring to the cruise control."

Casper leaned left and took a quick look at the dashboard. "Okay. We're going sixty-eight. So?"

"So we've been going exactly sixty-eight for the past hour."

"The speed limit is seventy."

"Yeah, I know. That's the idea. We stay a couple of miles below the speed limit we don't draw any attention from the cops."

"Either, we're driving through the desert in a moving billboard. I think we've gotten the attention of every cop the past two hundred miles."

"Yeah, but not the bad kind of attention."

"Over time, I've learned the hard way that any attention I've gotten from the cops has been bad, Either."

"That's because you've never been a famous author on tour before."

Casper shrugged and removed his tortoise-shell glasses. He started wiping the lenses and said, "Well, I don't know about famous. I do have a faithful and growing fan base…but I don't think I can, in good conscience, call myself famous…yet." He put his glasses back on and smiled at Either.

Either shook his head as he stared at the road outside. He grabbed his bottle of water from the drink holder, took a big gulp, and put the bottle back.

"My point about the cruise control was as an example of the overall quality and workmanship of this vehicle. The vehicle, I might remind you, that *I* procured for our little adventure."

"You're pretty generous with my money. Especially with money I don't have."

"You got it, Professor. And if you don't, you will soon. I just hope you fully appreciate the engineering marvel that is currently carrying your skinny white ass in total comfort down the highway."

Casper glanced around the interior of the Winnebago, forced to acknowledge the point. He nodded. "It is amazing. And I have no idea where they got these seats, but they sure are comfy."

"Sweet ride." Either beamed and snuck a couple of quick glances over his shoulder. "A real sweet ride indeed."

"When do I get to drive?"

"As soon as I say you can."

"Fine. Be an asshole."

"Man, what are you bitching about? You're never satisfied. You're riding in a Winnebago that has *your* picture plastered on the outside. I give you a world-class promotional campaign on wheels and you still ain't happy."

"Look, Either. I'm sorry. I didn't sleep very well."

"Well, judging by the snoring coming out of the *master* bedroom last night, the bedroom that you just *had to have*, you could have fucking fooled me."

"I said I was sorry."

"Ungrateful prick. You've got a 32-inch HDTV, surround sound, Blue Ray player, and Direct TV with the NFL package."

"Lighten up."

"You got a desk and leather chair so you can have a *dedicated space* to write, a queen size bed to sleep in and a tiled bathroom. Stainless steel appliances, mahogany cabinets, and at night when we park this thing, the sides actually slide out, thereby almost doubling the inside living space." Either slammed a fist on the console next to him. "And I just used the fucking word thereby. Fuck me. Now I'm even talking like you."

"If it's any consolation, you used it perfectly."

"Shut up!"

"Please don't yell at me."

"You'll be lucky if I don't smack you in the head." Either clenched the steering wheel. "*Please don't yell at me.* What a pussy." Either grabbed his water and took a long drink. He slammed the bottle back into the console. "Fuckwit."

"Are you done?" Casper whispered.

Either exhaled loudly, then nodded. "Yeah, I'm done."

"Good. Again, I'm sorry. I'm truly grateful for the Winnebago and everything else you've done for us."

"Thank you. All I wanted was for you to show a little appreciation."

"I'll try to do better." Casper placed the laptop on the console. "Want to take a look at the website?"

Either nodded and glanced back and forth between the road and the laptop. "I like the colors."

"They match the paint job on the Winnebago. I thought that would be a nice touch."

Either nodded again. "Yeah. Okay, I see you got your books on there. And the upcoming tour dates."

"Yeah."

"You got anything about why you're doing the tour? You know, what motivated you…no, wait…what inspired you to do it?"

"That's a great idea."

"I have my moments."

"No, it's perfect. I'm going to start working on it right now." Casper placed the laptop back in his lap. He removed his glasses and rubbed his eyes. "Let's see…what inspired this…journey? Hmmm."

"Just make sure you give them the non-felony version."

"Yeah, that's probably a good idea. I'll stick with something like my desire to go out into the world and meet…no, mingle with all my dedicated fans."

Either relaxed and settled back into the driver's seat.

"By this time tomorrow, we'll be heading into Vegas. Probably not the best place to kick off a book tour, but what do we care, right?"

Casper paused and looked over.

"The signing is at nine o'clock on Saturday, right?"

"Yeah. It's perfect. The jewelry store closes at nine. And they're closed on Sunday so nobody will even know the place has been hit until they open Monday morning. By then, we'll be in Oregon."

"I like your idea of staying with family-owned whenever possible."

"Yeah. If Mr. and Mrs. Smith's store gets knocked off they just chalk it up to bad luck and call their insurance company. We hit too many jewelry stores owned by the same corporation, pretty soon they're gonna start paying close attention, doubling up on their security…shit like that."

"Smart."

Either nodded and flashed that smile.

"Exactly."

He reached over and turned on the CD player. He turned it up and tapped the steering wheel to the beat.

"Is that Zappa?" Casper said.

"Yeah, Inca Roads. Eight minutes and forty-five seconds of perfection."

"He wrote some good songs."

"Shit," Either said. "Frank wasn't no songwriter. Jagger and Richards write songs. Lennon and McCartney were songwriters. Damn good ones too. But Zappa was a *composer*."

"Is there a difference?"

"There's a huge difference."

Either turned up the volume.

"Thanks for the clarification," Casper said, refocusing on the laptop.

Either let the music wash over him as he steered the massive vehicle doing exactly sixty-eight miles an hour down the flat stretch of highway. He waved back to a passing vehicle that was holding up a copy of one of Casper's books in the back window. Either nudged Casper who looked up, then smiled and waved at the car's passengers. Either settled deeper into the comfortable leather as the guitar solo began.

"This should be a movie," he whispered.

"What's that?" Casper said, glancing up from his work.

"All this. This should be a movie. My *life* should be a movie."

Casper considered the idea, then shrugged. "How about a book?"

"What?"

"Your life…as a book."

"A book? You out of your mind?"

"What's wrong with it being a book?"

"Nobody reads books any more. Maybe bored housewives looking to get their panties wet reading shit like yours. They're the only ones. Nobody else, except for the fuckwits and the old."

"Millions of people of all ages read books all the time. *I* read books all the time."

Either paused, then glanced over at Casper.

"Funny, you don't look that old."

Casper scowled at Either, then went back to work.

"Fuckwit."

"Takes one to know one, Professor."

5

*C*asper stepped off the Winnebago into a blinding sunset and shimmering heat. Hands on hips, he scanned the back lot of the mini-mall and grimaced as the smell of garbage baking wafted in on the breeze. Either, in the process of adjusting a small device attached to his belt, stepped down from the vehicle and glanced around. He noticed a homeless man inching closer, eyeing the Winnebago.

"Okay, dude. Off you go." Either took a step towards the man, who had stopped and was keeping a close eye on both of them. "Nothing to see here. And the security system is wired directly to the cops." Either clicked a button on the key ring, and the vehicle beeped.

"Bullshit," the man said.

Either laughed. "Nothing gets past you, huh? Okay, you caught me. It ain't wired to the cops. But *I'll* know. And that prospect alone should be enough to scare the shit out of you. And if I find so much as a scratch on it when I come back, I'm gonna find you and mess up that lovely fashion statement you got going on there."

"Go fuck yourself." The man spit near the Winnebago and staggered away muttering to himself.

"Cautionary tale?" Casper said.

"Yeah. Tough country."

Either shook his head as he watched him walk away, then glanced around. "Well, it ain't Mandalay Bay, but it'll do." He started fiddling with the gadget attached to his belt.

"What is that thing?" Casper said.

"Portable laser measuring device," Either said, nodding. "C'mon it stinks back here. Let's go join the civilized world."

"Hey, it was the only space I could find big enough to park this thing."

"Did I say anything? Or blame you for parking in the wrong spot?" Either started walking towards the front of the mini-mall. "A little touchy today, aren't we?"

"I'm just nervous," Casper said. "I always get nervous before signings."

Either stopped and shook his head.

"What?" Casper said.

"The signing. I completely forgot."

Either unlocked the Winnebago, went inside, then soon returned with two boxes and a portable dolly. He relocked the vehicle and stacked the boxes on the dolly.

"Since you're supposed to be here to do a book signing, it might be a good idea to actually bring some along for you to sign."

"Yeah," Casper said, laughing. "Probably would be."

They headed up a ramp that led to the main walkway along the front of the mini-mall. As they reached the edge of the building, Either stopped and adjusted the laser device on his belt.

"Okay," he said, his voice lowered. He scanned the area to make sure they were alone. "I need you to head up the walkway until you reach the far end of the bookstore."

"Can I ask why?"

"I'd be shocked if you didn't, Professor." Either draped an arm around Casper's shoulder. "First, you gotta lighten up. You're just here to do a book signing. And you're a bit early, so you're just wandering around outside, getting the lay of the land, getting ready for your show. Got it?"

"Yeah," Casper said. "I got it. I'm okay."

"Of course you're okay. You're gonna do great." Either said, as if talking to a small child.

Casper ignored the insult and waited.

"The bookstore starts at this end of the building." Either cocked his head slightly to the left. "That wall right there, in fact. What we're gonna do is get some measurements on where the various stores stop and start."

Either stopped talking as a couple walked by. He beamed at them, brushed imaginary lint from Casper's lapel, then continued in a whisper.

"Even though the internal bones of these places are the same, they all got different stores in different sizes. That means they gotta do some rerouting of the ductwork and maybe the security systems. Especially the security system inside the jewelry store."

"And?"

"And we gotta have the measurements of where each store stops and starts. When we're crawling around inside later, with the spiders and mice, it'll be nice to know where we are, what to look for, what to expect, shit like that. I thought you did this for a living."

"Residential only. This is my first commercial building."

"Same shit. Just like cars and women. You able to drive one, you can handle them all. Some are just bigger and more dangerous than others."

"So what do you want me to do?"

"I need you to walk up there, real casual…like you haven't got a care in the world, because you don't." He gave Casper's shoulder a gentle squeeze. "And when you get to the end of the bookstore, stop and just turn and look out at the street. Don't wave, don't point, just turn."

"I can do that," Casper said.

"One would hope. After that, I need you to move until you see where the second store starts. Should only be a couple feet, but make sure you get it right. It's a Victoria's Secret, so take your time. Do some casual window shopping, just like any other horny guy would be doing. When you got it, just turn and face the street again real casual, like you're a tourist."

Casper nodded and adjusted his sports coat.

"Then you're gonna find where the third store starts; that's the one we want. The jewelry store. Find where it starts, turn to the street. Walk to the end of the store, stop, and face the street. Easy as shit."

"It sounds like a lot of unnecessary work. Why don't you just go inside and walk the stores?"

"Because I don't want my face on every damn video surveillance system they got inside."

Casper nodded, then glanced around. "Yeah, that makes sense. Good thinking. You think they have cameras out here?"

Either thought about it. "Doubtful. Well, maybe. But why do we care? We're supposed to be here. Our favorite romance writer is here to sign some books and dazzle his fans."

"I'm still nervous."

"Well, if it makes you feel any better, you ain't doing much for my mood. Now get going. And relax. Smile and nod your head at all the friendly people as you walk by."

Either watched Casper turn and slowly roll the dolly stacked with boxes of books down the walkway. He placed a hand on his hip near the laser and waited. Casper stopped walking, turned to the street. Either tapped the laser and checked the readout. He nodded casually at Casper, who then resumed his stroll. They repeated the process until Either had stored all six readings. He began strolling in Casper's direction, stopping about halfway up the walkway to lean down and smile at a baby in a stroller. He stood and smiled at the young mother pushing the stroller.

"Cute kid," Either said.

"Thanks," she said. "I'm sorry, I hate to be rude and rush off, but I need to get him to the babysitter. I just saw that one of my favorite authors is doing a book signing here later on."

"Oh, are you a fan of Casper?"

"You know him?" she said, wide-eyed.

"I'm his manager."

"Really? I just love him. God, I just love his books. They make me so...well, you know." She managed a nervous giggle.

"Exactly. I certainly do."

Either glanced at the woman's left hand, devoid of wedding ring, then up at her face. She was staring off into the distance and her tongue rested on the corner of her lips.

"Well, the signing starts at nine, so make sure you're back by then."

"Oh, I'll be here." She waved and headed down the walkway towards the parking lot.

Either admired her and decided that the book signings might actually make a valuable contribution after all. Good looking women getting all hot and bothered listening to the Professor recite his clumsy metaphors from behind those lame-ass tortoise shell glasses. Could be good, he thought. If he could figure out a way to make the time, make it happen without putting them behind schedule, get in the way of why they were here in the first place. ..all work and no play or so they said. So why not try to spend a few hours with some bored housewives looking to have some fun?

Especially if Casper was laying all the groundwork.

Shit…they'd wind up in Either's lap already revved up.

Ready to go.

Either's concentration broke as Casper approached. His smile faded.

"What were you talking with her about?"

"Her? Oh, I was just helping you sell a few books."

"Is she coming later?"

Either stared off into the distance and whispered, "I sure hope so."

"What?"

"Nothing."

Either looked at Casper and nodded at the bookstore's entrance.

"C'mon, Professor. Let's go sell some books."

6

"*U*sually, we don't get a lot of indie authors doing signings. They mostly do e-books or they're not very good writers and I can't even give their stuff away."

Either worked hard to stay focused on what the manager was saying. He was dying to know what Casper had discovered.

"But when you called, I checked Casper out and learned that he sells pretty well and has a small but loyal following."

"Yeah," Either said, glancing towards the hallway leading to the storeroom and offices. "We think this tour is really going to help the general public discover him."

"It's an amazing promotional idea," she said. "And the paint job on that bus is amazing."

"It's a Winnebago." Either beamed at her. "And thank you. This whole tour was my idea."

"Well, I think it's pure genius," she said. "And the book industry certainly needs all the help it can get these days."

"Yes, it's a difficult period indeed," Either said, sneaking another peek down the hallway. "But as I always say, when people find themselves in a place devoid of hope, one never knows what incredible opportunities might exist right next door."

"A truly valuable sentiment," she said, placing a hand on Either's arm.

"Let's hope so." Either beamed at her.

She glanced up the hallway.

"He's been gone quite a while. Do you think he's okay?"

"He's been fighting a stomach bug ever since we stopped at a roadside diner for lunch. Maybe I should go check on him." Either glanced at his watch. "It looks like we have a few minutes before he goes on."

"Of course," she said. "Tell him to take all the time he needs."

"You're too kind," Either said, heading towards the hallway.

He walked to the end of the hall, glanced around but found no sign of Casper. He located the men's room, and found Casper washing his hands.

"Everything cool, Professor?"

"More than cool, my man. More than cool."

Either glanced around the bathroom.

"Don't worry," Casper said. "We're alone." He began rearranging his hair and glanced at Either through the mirror. "How's the crowd?"

"What the hell are you talking about? Who gives a shit how the crowd is?"

"I do."

"Jesus. I've created a monster."

"You should be nice to the man holding the bookstore's password to the security system."

"What?"

"If this is how they run the rest of their business, it's no wonder they're going broke."

Casper stood back from the mirror and tugged his jacket's sleeves. He put his tortoise shell glasses on and admired himself.

"How do I look?"

"Like you should be working here. How'd you get your hands on the password?"

"I walked into the manager's office, opened the front drawer of her desk, and there it was."

"You're kidding, right?"

"We don't even have to break anything getting in. We do the signing, drive back to the RV campground, and ride our bikes back over here when we're ready. Once we're in, we can take all the time we want."

"Did you find anywhere with easy access to the ductwork?"

"Right above her desk is an air vent. She's got one of those drop ceilings in there. We take a couple panels out, get up there, and work our way down to the jewelry store. I'm betting we'll find the electrical to their alarm system up there somewhere. Probably their video surveillance system, too."

"Can it be that easy?"

"I think so. It'll be a long crawl along the ductwork, but it'll be worth it."

"About a hundred thirty feet."

"Well, there you go. Okay, I'm ready."

They exited the bathroom and headed towards the entrance back into the store. Casper hung back. Either stopped and looked at Casper.

"What are you doing?"

"Waiting for my introduction, of course. You gonna do it?"

Either scoffed. "Yeah, right."

"Some business manager you are."

Either headed into the store and spoke briefly with the manager before heading to the back of the store behind the small but eager crowd. He leaned against the wall and counted about thirty people, all women, except for one young man clutching one of Casper's books across his chest.

Either listened to the manager's gushing introduction and the loud burst of applause that followed. Casper played the humble 'I'm so honored to be here tonight' to the hilt – cleared his throat, sipped water, adjusted those annoying fucking glasses - then started reading from one of his books.

It was the one about a returning war vet who falls in love with his therapist. Then she gets drafted and ends up captured in some shithole country, so he reenlists and volunteers for a mission to save her hot little ass. As they're making their escape, they're getting it on hot and heavy in the back of a cargo plane when a missile shoots the thing down and they plunge to their deaths without missing a stroke. What the hell was the title? *Deep Inside Above the Fray*? That was it. Casper was always bragging about how it was a book that had everything. Yeah, Either had said, everything except a coherent storyline and believable characters.

But, man, this group was eating it up, hanging on every word. Either scanned the crowd and located the young housewife with the stroller he'd met earlier, in the front row. Her eyes never left Casper as he worked his way through what Either considered a clumsy, rambling section about how to keep an ammo belt from gouging naked thighs. He moved to a side wall and studied her. She was leaning forward in her chair staring intensely at Casper as he droned on, elbows on knees, clenched hands propping up her chin.

Horny?

Without a doubt.

Available to him?

Not a fucking chance.

Either saw a woman approaching him from one side. He flashed that smile at her and waited.

"Betty tells me you're his business manager."

Either looked her over and noticed the cameraman standing behind her. A cute blonde, probably mid-twenties. Eager to move her career forward, he decided, but already tired around the eyes.

"I am. And you are?"

"I'm Sally Gilbert from Channel 13."

"How can I help you?"

"I need three minutes for tomorrow morning's Sunday in Vegas. And this," she said, spreading her arms to encompass the room, "is the most interesting thing I have on my list of potentials."

"In all of Vegas? Are you shitting me?"

"I know. Sad, but true. I've got plenty of drunken tourists beating each other up on The Strip and tons of petty crime. But it's a slow weekend for major shows and not one celebrity has been busted for drugs or flashed her cooch getting out of a limo."

"What happened to 'what happens in Vegas, stays in Vegas'?"

"Hey, it's a local show."

Either laughed.

"So you want to interview Casper?"

"I do," she said, watching Casper who was now standing and waving an arm as he read. "And I thought we could get a shot of him outside the Winnebago. It's a pretty cool concept...the endless book tour angle."

"Sure. We'd be happy to help."

"That's great," she said. "Just meet us outside when you finish up here."

"Perfect," Either said. "And then..."

Sally's defense system switched on. She stared hard at Either. "Then what?"

"Well, I was just wondering what you're doing later on, that's all."

"You mean, who I'm doing."

"Well, I wouldn't want to presume, but who knows what the night may bring, right?"

She continued to stare, but a small smile appeared.

"Look no offense, but there's no way that's gonna happen."

"Excuse me for showing interest," Either said. "I was only-"

"Not a chance in hell."

"I heard you the first time."

Sally glanced back at Casper.

"But him...now he's got a real shot."

7

*B*oth bicycles left the sidewalk, hugged the back wall that ran the length of the mini-mall then rolled to a stop behind the bookstore. Casper got off and leaned his bike against the wall. He approached the back door and removed a piece of paper from his pants pocket. He reached for the keypad of the alarm device next to the door, then paused when he heard Either's voice.

"Gloves."

Casper turned and held up his hands. "Way ahead of you. Now keep quiet."

"Well, excuse me for paying attention to details."

Casper glanced at the piece of paper, then tapped a long sequence into the keypad. The panel flashed green. He opened the door and held it as Either rolled both bikes inside. Casper stepped inside and closed the door. He folded the paper and put it back in his pocket.

"It's a very safe password," Casper said, laughing. "Lots of special characters and almost impossible to hack. But I guess that doesn't mean much when you leave it written down in plain sight."

"Exactly," Either said. "I'm a bit worried about that camera right above the back door."

"We're fine," Casper said. "We were only out there for a few seconds. It's just one of about two dozen cameras they've got ringing the building. And I'm sure the image is showing up on some monitor as a quarter-screen."

"Quarter-screen? English, please." Either unzipped his backpack and examined the contents.

"What are you doing? Shouldn't you wait to unpack until we get inside the jewelry store?"

"Looking for my gum."

Either held up the pack and offered it to Casper.

"I'm good," Casper said, unzipping his jacket. "A quarter-screen is just what it says. Rather than spring for an individual monitor for each camera, most security companies, especially this one that pays their employees about ten bucks an hour, save money by feeding four cameras into one monitor. Trust me, the guy monitoring that camera would have to be staring right at that specific screen at the exact moment we went in. And even if he was watching, what's he got? Some bookstore employee punching in the password and going in the store. No alarm triggered, no problem. Perfect time for him to get back to his nap."

"Yeah. 3:30 in the morning, and he's sitting there staring at blank TV screens." Either chewed, pondering the implications of that career choice, then shook his head. "Man, what a shitty job."

"Yeah," Casper said. "I'm not worried about him. Let's say we go see what challenges the jewelry store has in store for us."

They entered the manager's office. Casper turned the lights on.

"What are you doing?"

Either scrambled to the door and turned them back off.

In the darkness, he heard Casper's whisper.

"Dumbass."

"What?"

"Turn the fucking lights back on."

"Man, you trying to get caught? We ain't even got started and here you are announcing our presence."

"The office doesn't have any windows."

"What? Oh. You sure?"

"Just turn them back on."

Either did as he was told. In the bright light, Either scanned the room, then nodded. "Sure. That makes sense. This office is built in the middle of a big storeroom. Why would it have windows?"

"Why indeed?" Casper stared up at the ceiling. "How do you want to get up there?"

"You want to get on my shoulders? Then after you're up there, you can pull me up."

"That sounds like a lot of work. All those books on shelves out there. There's gotta be a ladder somewhere."

Either nodded and left the office. A few minutes later he returned rolling a large ladder with wheels. Casper smiled and nodded.

"How's this?" Either said, rolling the ladder to the center of the office.

"Perfect. It's almost like they knew we were coming."

Either laughed and climbed the ladder until he could reach the ceiling tiles. He removed one and handed it down to Casper. Either turned on a small flashlight and poked his head through the opening. Moments later, he climbed down, laughing.

"Unbelievable," he said, rolling the ladder a few feet to the left. "Remember when our boy Jack was being interviewed by that trade magazine?"

"Whitehead? Sure."

"And was going on about how all the tradesmen loved working on his buildings?"

"Yeah, he said they were designed with maintenance in mind," Casper said.

"Well, he wasn't lying. The crawlspace is wide and high and runs the length of the building. We may have to hunch over a bi,t but we can scoot down to the jewelry store in less than a minute."

Two minutes later, after climbing the ladder and stepping onto the crawlspace that ran alongside all the building's electrical, plumbing and ductwork, they stood directly above Jewel's Diamond Desert Rocks Emporium.

"Same cheap-ass ceiling tiles," Either said.

Casper began examining the wiring in the immediate area. "Son of a bitch. We are definitely leading a charmed life, Either."

"You got good news?"

"Take a look at this." Casper held up a collection of three individual wires bundled together.

"Okay." Either shone the flashlight on the bundle. "What am I looking at?"

"These three wires are each connected to a different component of the store's security systems. Definitely the front door lock and the motion detectors, and probably a keypad that controls access into the office where the safe is."

"Shit. They got motion sensors?"

"I'm sure they do."

"Well, that doesn't seem fair," Either said.

Casper laughed. "Don't worry about it." He held the bundle of wires closer to the light. "You see how all three wires are individually connected to this piece of plastic, but then only one bigger wire comes out the other side?"

"I do. But I'm gonna need a little more, Professor."

"You know what a power strip is, right?"

"Sure. That's the thing you buy for your house when you run out of places to plug shit in."

"Exactly." Casper shook his head. "Shit. Now you got me saying it. The security system they use is based on the same concept. These three wires all control a different part of the system and, if anything happens with any one part, a signal is sent through this one bigger wire here."

"Sent where?"

"To the place where big guys with guns sit around and wait for people like you and me to fuck up."

"But we're not going to do that, are we?"

"No, my friend, we are not." Casper stretched his legs out to get more comfortable. "A lot of the systems use cellular networks, but this one uses a landline to communicate."

"Landline? Like if I had a regular phone in the house instead of just using my cellphone?"

"Exactly." Casper shook his head again. "Damn, I gotta stop saying that. Now if this system was controlled by a cellular network, I'd just redirect the signal to an alternate cell tower."

"Sure. Just build your own cell tower, whatever the hell that is."

"It's already built," Casper said. He reached into his backpack and removed various wires, clamps and a small pair of pliers.

"What are you talking about?"

"I already built it, and it's ready to go if we ever need it," Casper said.

"What?" Either said, baffled.

"It's on top of the Winnebago. But it's small and impossible to see from the ground." Casper removed a small device from the backpack.

"What's that?"

"That, my friend, is a voltage meter. You see, if you cut the big wire or any of the three individual wires, the signal going to the big guys with guns gets interrupted."

"And that would be bad."

"Yes. That would be bad, Either."

"Hey, you don't have to get all snotty and talk to me like I'm a mental midget. I'm trying to learn here."

"Sorry. Anyway, security companies monitor these links by checking for a specific voltage. And as long as the voltage signal doesn't change, we could be having a toga party in here and they wouldn't have a clue."

"So how do we disable the system without interrupting the signal?"

"Now that's a trade secret."

"And you're not going to tell me?"

"Exactly."

Casper laughed as he turned his back and began working on the wiring. A few minutes later, he turned back around and showed Either the modification he'd made. Either examined the small device attached to the large wire, about two feet above the point where the three individual wires were connected.

"I've bypassed the main connection and connected a separate signal that provides a constant signal of the correct voltage." Casper slid forward and grabbed a pair of wire cutters from the backpack.

"That's it?" Either said.

"That's it. Now all I need to do is cut the wire below the bypass to disable all three systems." Casper snipped the large wire and sat back. "Hear that?"

"I don't hear anything," Either beamed. "That's a good sign, right?"

"Yeah. Okay, superstar, you're up."

"About time," Either said as he reached down to grab one of the ceiling tiles. "When you get down there, just remember that there's enough light to still through off shadows. So stay low."

"Got it," Casper said, refilling his backpack. "You start working on the safe and I'll check to see if they're dumb enough to leave shit in their cases overnight."

"Don't start smashing the glass."

"Jesus, do I look stupid?"

"Only when you're wearing those fucking glasses."

Bickering and scowling, they climbed through the opening in the ceiling and dropped quietly onto the thick carpet below. Either headed straight to the back office, where he assumed the safe was located. Gently testing the door handle, as if expecting to get a static-shock, he beamed as the door swung open. He stood in the doorway listening, his head cocked to one side, then stepped inside and closed the door. Another office without windows, he noted. He flipped the lights on, and there it was, sitting right there. Waiting for him. Big one. And old.

"Come to papa," he said, staring lovingly at the safe.

"What the fuck do you think you're doing here?"

Either jumped at the sound of the deep voice. He screamed, wheeled around, and raised the flashlight to defend himself. "You prick. Don't do that."

Casper laughed and sat down in one the chairs. "Sorry, I couldn't resist. Wow, that was good."

"Last guy did that to me is now eating through a tube." Either glared at Casper. "Don't do that."

"Relax," Casper said. "Just thought I'd come in here and watch you work. The cases are all empty."

"Well, that means we've probably got a very full safe here."

"What's it look like?"

"Piece of cake. It's an old TL 15."

"English, please."

Either began emptying his backpack. He removed a portable acetylene torch and tossed the backpack on the desk.

"Safes are given different ratings based on how strong they are at keeping people like me out. TL means a safe is tool-resistant. That means it's been designed to prevent me getting in by using your basic power tools, drills, shit like that. TR means it's resistant to torches. A TRTL rating combines both, and a TXTL means it's resistant to torches, tools, and *explosives.*"

"And this one is a TL, only resistant to tools?"

"Yup."

"What's the fifteen stand for?"

"That's a measure of time. How long the safe can stand up to a full-on assault." Either lit the portable torch and beamed.

"How long is it going to take?"

"Bet you a hundred bucks I'm in less than five minutes," Either said, getting to work.

"You're on." Casper checked his watch and leaned back in his chair.

Four minutes and thirty seven seconds later Either turned the torch off and set it on the desk. He reached into the backpack and removed a small crowbar. He wedged it into the side of the safe's door and stepped back as it slowly opened. He placed the crowbar and torch in the backpack and beamed at Casper.

"Son of a bitch," Casper said, staring wide-eyed into the safe.

"Okay, Professor," Either said, removing a large zippered sack from the backpack. "Stay focused. No counting, no examining the goods. Just fill the bag, zip it tight, and we're out of here."

Casper nodded and began filling the sack with dozens of small envelopes, bundles of cash, and a large collection of gold coins. After he filled the first bag, he handed it to Either, who gave him a second. Casper filled that one halfway. Either closed the door to the safe and nodded at Casper. They both took a final look around the office and, satisfied that they'd left no clues, switched the light off and reentered the store. Either found a small three-step footstool and placed it under the open ceiling space. He reached into the backpack and removed a length of rope.

"What are you doing?" Casper said.

"Confusing the hell out of them," he said, grinning.

He tied the rope to the footstool, then extended his arm in a 'you first' gesture to Casper, who took two steps up and climbed back up through the ceiling onto the crawlspace. Either tossed the rope up through the hole in the ceiling. Seconds late,r it fell back onto the floor.

"Hey, Professor."

"What?" Casper said.

"Pay attention and catch the fucking thing."

Either tossed the rope again. Casper caught it and moved to one side as Either climbed up. Either took the rope and carefully pulled the footstool up through the ceiling. He placed the footstool on the crawlspace, then replaced the ceiling tile. He folded the footstool and slid it in front of him as he moved down the crawlspace on his knees. About thirty feet away, he slid the folded footstool onto the top of the ductwork, then worked his way back to Casper who was already fiddling with the bypass he'd created earlier.

"What are you doing?" Either said.

"Just getting in the spirit of confusing the hell out of them." Casper laughed and shook his head. "I'm going to reconnect all three sub-systems, then remove the bypass."

Either laughed. "Unbelievable. There won't be a trace of anything. You know what it's like?"

"What?"

"It's like that old brainteaser where they find a guy hanging from the ceiling with no ladder or any way for him to get high enough off the ground to hang himself."

"Yeah, I remember that one. A big block of ice that melts. And after the floor dries, there aren't any clues. Yeah, this is similar. Good one, Either."

"Man, even when you're paying me a compliment, it sounds like you just watched some chimp manage to use the toilet and flush."

"You're too sensitive," Casper said. He glanced around, checked his backpack to make sure all the pockets were zipped tight, then looked at Either. "You ready?"

"Yeah, let's get out of here before the sun comes up. Probably not a good idea to be seen walking out of the bookstore in broad daylight."

Casper nodded and began working his way back along the crawlspace. Either followed close behind.

"You know what I was thinking?" Casper said.

"What's that?"

"The first thing the insurance company is going to think about when they do their investigation."

"Inside job."

"Yup. I know that's what I'd be thinking."

"Gotta love old technology."

"Yeah, everybody wants the latest and greatest until they have to pay for it."

Either laughed. "And everybody is always convinced that it'll never happen to them."

"Makes our job a lot easier," Casper said, rapidly working his way along the crawlspace.

"Exactly."

They replaced the ceiling tiles in the bookstore, returned the ladder to where Either had found it, and slowly opened the door that led outside. Satisfied they were alone and unseen they closed the door, reset the alarm code, then rode their bikes back through the warm late-night air.

8

*O*ne eye open, then the other. Head pounding. Some asshole pounding on the door. Jerry sat up in bed, almost threw up, then coughed. A familiar voice from the hallway.

"Hey, Jerry. You alive?"

"Go away."

"C'mon, man, it's almost eleven. We gotta get downstairs before the buffet line winds around the block. Then we're gonna play some blackjack. C'mon. Time's a wastin'."

Jerry checked the clock next to the bed. Shit, it was almost eleven. He hadn't slept this late in years. But then, it had been years since he'd drunk a bottle and a half of Jack Daniels.

"C'mon. After that, we're gonna head to the pool and check out all the babes wearing dental floss between their butt cheeks."

Babes? Jerry shook his head. The guy was right out of the 1950's. Probably thought *Mad Men* was a reality show. Who was he again? Bobby's cousin? No, Fred's brother-in-law.

"I'll meet you guys down there later," Jerry said, stretching back out under the thick cotton sheets.

"Okay, but don't take too long. Everything that happens in Vegas can't stay in Vegas if nothing happens, right?"

Jerry heard the laughter on the other side of the door; then it got quiet. Before the hangover, Vegas had sounded like a pretty good way to start his suspension. Get out of town, cool off and just chill for a few days. Besides, what would he be doing if he wasn't here? Probably waking up in his bed alone and hung over.

Two months suspension without pay and another round of mandatory anger management classes.

Anger management?

Really?

With all the shit he'd seen the past five years, the Bureau should consider itself lucky he wasn't redlining every day. Unbelievable shit. But all too real. Between the white collar scumbags with every advantage life could offer, yet still feeling the need to steal even more for themselves, and the truly criminally insane…like the guy who walked into a McDonald's thinking it was a bank, baked on meth, holding a gun powerful enough to bring down an elephant, guns the FBI wouldn't even issue to their own agents because they were too dangerous…the meth head screaming at the Hispanic kid working the counter to empty the register, *no dye packs…got it, motherfucker? no fucking dye packs*…poor kid, barely spoke English and kept saying, *Big Mac?...you don't want Big Mac?*…the meth head standing there, gun shaking in his hand, screaming, starting to lose it…the kid staring back, scared to death by the gun and the wild-eyed beast holding it…the kid starts crying he's so fucking scared, manages to get out *'Would you like fries with-'* before the guy shoots him, elephant gun blows a hole the size of a softball straight through him as well as the manager standing right behind him. Guy walks out, forgets to take the cash from the register the kid had handed him.

Local cops picked him up later that night, fried out of his mind, and found out he'd sold his kid for an ounce of crystal…sold his own fucking kid. If he'd been in the room when the guy confessed that he wasn't sure what he'd have done. But he was pretty sure his response wouldn't have been one of the techniques they teach you in anger management class.

Anger management?

Yeah, the whole job was all about managing your anger. And, truth be told, he probably shouldn't have beaten that witness up. The guy had given him some lip, called him a cocksucking pig…probably should have just walked out and let somebody else deal with him.

But, shit, two months without pay for that?

What's the big deal?

Just one more scumbag leaving a trail of slime behind him.

Besides the scumbag was already out of the hospital, and Jerry was almost certain he was faking that limp.

Anger management classes?

What a joke.

It wasn't like he'd shot the fucking guy.

Jerry climbed out of bed, ordered room service, and switched on the TV. Unable to decide whether to shower before his coffee was delivered, he sat down in a chair and stared at the screen. Some painted Winnebago with a picture on the side of the same guy being interviewed by a cute reporter. Some romance book writer who was starting an endless book tour. Just driving around the country in a Winnebago, promoting his books. Jerry thought about that idea and decided there were probably worse ways to make a living. Like dealing with scumbag meth heads who carried elephant guns and sold their kids.

Jerry studied the woman doing the interview. Definitely had the look and personality. But she was young. And eager. Probably her first real TV job, getting some weird assignments like interviewing a romance writer in a parking lot late at night, but still real experience she could use later on to get herself into a bigger market like New York or L.A.

Jerry shook his head. *You're on suspension, so just turn your brain off. Always analyzing, sizing things up, making assumptions about people…*the job just did that to you. What difference did it make to him where some TV reporter eventually landed? She could marry a pit boss and start pumping out kids for all he cared.

How long was that coffee gonna take to get here?

Jerry reached for the remote, about to change channels, when the camera pulled back to show the entire Winnebago. Jerry stared at the screen, confused by what he saw. Couldn't be him. But, son of a bitch, he'd recognize that smile anywhere. He watched the guy approach the writer and whisper something to him. The writer nodded and the guy stepped back, but still in the shot, beaming at the interviewer, smiling for the camera.

What the hell is going on here?

Either Ore?

Several questions immediately came to mind, but one in particular kept circling back.

What on earth was the best jewel thief he'd ever seen doing on a book tour?

Jerry would have bet his two months' pay it wasn't to sell books.

He found his cellphone and located the stored number.

"Hey, Sam. It's Jerry. Yeah…Vegas is good…broke even so far…sorry to bother you at home on a Sunday, but I need a favor. I know I'm on suspension. But this isn't really work. Besides, I'd do this one for free. Remember a guy named Either Ore? Jewelry thief that got sent up a few years ago. Yeah, that's the one. Well, he's out. Do me a favor and let me know when he got out, what he's been up to since then…yeah, you know the drill. What's that? You're damn right it's personal." Jerry laughed. "Yeah, I'll do that. Just give me a call when you got something for me. Thanks, Sam. Later."

He headed to the bathroom to pee, then popped four Advil. He heard a knock on the door and let the guy with his breakfast in. He signed the check, poured coffee, and devoured a piece of bacon. He took a sip of coffee and felt a bit better. Munching on an English muffin, he made another call.

"Hi. It's me. Yeah, long time no talk. Bet you thought you were done with me…sorry, not my problem. I need a favor. Nothing you can't handle. I don't care. What? How much longer? Tell you what, you do a good job on this one, maybe we can talk about that. No, I don't have any details yet. I'll need a couple days to put some things together, but I just wanted to tell you to clear your calendar…for how long? Until I tell you we're finished…that's not very nice."

Jerry laughed into the phone.

"Well, apart from all that, how have you been?"

9

"*D*amn," Casper said. "That was good. How'd I look?"

Either changed channels to *House Hunters*.

"Jesus, for the fourth time in the last five minutes, you were fine. Apart from the glasses."

"I just wish we had a bit more time. I think I had a real shot with that reporter."

Either scoffed.

"Yeah, you had a shot with her. Please."

"You saw those women at the signing last night."

Either nodded, but refused to comment.

"And?" Casper said.

"And I'm sick of talking about you and your books." His voice dropped to a whisper. "Why don't we do something more important, like take a look inside those two bags?"

Casper nodded and smiled.

"Yeah, good idea. It's kinda like Christmas, isn't it?"

Either walked to the oven, opened it, and retrieved both bags.

"We gotta find a better hiding place. Some night you're liable to forget they're in there and start cooking dinner."

"It would still be an improvement over your cooking."

"Go grab a towel," Either said.

"What do you need a towel for?"

"So when we empty the envelopes that we hope are all filled with diamonds, they don't go bouncing off the table and all over the Winnebago."

"Good idea. Smart."

Casper headed to the bathroom and returned with a clean towel. He spread it out and sat down at the table, anxious and excited.

"Hang on," Either said. "Gloves."

Casper nodded and they both pulled on a pair of their surgical gloves. Either reached into one of the bags and selected several small white envelopes. He opened one and poured the contents onto the towel. Three diamonds sparkled on the terrycloth.

"Nice," Either said.

He picked up a jeweler's loupe and examined one of the rocks.

"These are about a carat each. Pretty nice quality. Amir will probably give us a couple grand each for these."

"Who's Amir?"

"He's my favorite fence. He's down in L.A. Best in the business."

"Can we trust him?"

"Trust him? The guy spends his whole life dealing stolen gold and diamonds. Who the fuck's he gonna tell?"

"Well, you know…if something happened and he got squeezed by the cops."

"There are still some people working in this industry who live by the code and know how to keep their mouth shut."

Either glared at Casper. Casper stayed silent as he picked up an envelope and emptied it on the towel. Either paused to watch.

"Wow," Casper said. "That's a big rock. Gotta be at least three carats." He picked up his own loupe and examined the stone. "I can't see anything wrong with this one. Take a look."

Either gently held the stone up to his loupe. "Beautiful. Great clarity. This guy certainly knows his diamonds. This would retail for seventy, maybe eighty grand."

"What sort of deal can we get with this guy, Amir?"

"That's the good thing about him. Amir's a total pro and doesn't try to screw you. As long as the stuff is good quality and the cops aren't following us into his office, he'll give us twenty-five, thirty percent of retail."

"That's good. Most of those guys try to give you ten, fifteen percent and expect you to be happy with it."

"Yeah, well, Amir and me go way back."

Either emptied another envelope. Several smaller diamonds landed on the towel.

"We've had some good times. He's Muslim, but he likes his booze and smokes a little hash. But what he really loves is pussy. No waiting for seventy virgins in heaven for this guy. A total pussy hound."

"From the Middle East?"

"Nah, he's originally from India, but Muslims over there are in the minority and surrounded by Hindus. He came over here for school, discovered he had a knack for gold and diamonds, and never left."

Either picked up one of the smaller diamonds and examined it through the loupe.

"You wouldn't believe some of the women he's had. And I'm talking about some *famous* women. Actresses, musicians, business executives, even a couple of politicians."

"Politicians?" Casper said, frowning. "Why even bother?"

"Turns the man on. He figures they been screwing us for so long, it's nice to be able to return the favor once in a while."

Casper laughed. "Maybe we'll get a chance to hang out with him when we get to L.A."

"Doubtful," Either said, emptying another envelope. "He's pretty much gone underground these days. You moved as much stolen product as this guy does, you'd be keeping a low profile too."

Either picked up another large diamond.

"But that don't keep him from chasing pussy. Man's a fucking legend."

"Let's see what we've got in this one." Casper reached inside the second bag and dropped several gold coins on the towel. "There's a surprise."

"Kruggerands. Nice. They go for around fifteen hundred each. How many?"

Casper counted the coins.

"Looks like thirty. No need to fence these."

"That's right," Either said. "A normal part of any man's investment portfolio. What else is in there?"

Casper began removing the contents.

"Let's see, we got your usual suspects, like high-end watches, bracelets, necklaces…"

"Find me a nice pair of diamond earrings. We still owe Jimmy for the set of blueprints." Either beamed at Casper. "And, yes, they're coming out of your share."

Casper stared down at the towel, now covered with diamonds, gold coins and assorted pieces of jewelry.

"Sure. Who cares?"

They both jumped when they heard the knock on the door.

"Shit," Either said, heading to the bathroom. He returned with a fresh towel and laid it on top of the other.

Casper waited, then headed towards the door.

"Hey, Professor."

Casper stopped and turned his head back to Either. Either nodded at Casper's hands.

"Gloves."

"Shit. I almost forgot."

He pulled his gloves off, eased the door part way open and stuck his head out. A woman clutching one of his books stared up at him.

"It is you," she said. "I can't believe it. We just pulled in and I saw your picture on the side, and just had to come over. I'm so sorry to disturb you, but could you sign a book for me? I'm about halfway through, and I just *love* it."

Casper smiled, glanced back at the scowling Either, then turned back to the woman. "I'd be happy to." He reached into the pocket of his shirt and removed a black Sharpie. "Who should I make it out to?"

"Josie. I'm Josie Walters. It's so nice to meet you…I mean, who would have thought that I'd run into you like this?"

"Who indeed?" Casper said, handing her the book.

"To Josie," she said, reading the inscription, "may all your dreams be hot and sweet." She looked up at Casper. "If I keep reading your books, I'm sure they will." She glanced away, then looked back at him. "Look, if you're not doing anything later, maybe we could get together for a drink or something?" She glanced around Casper and snuck a peek into the Winnebago. "Or now, perhaps?"

Casper considered the idea, glanced back at Either, then smiled at her.

"I would love to, but my manager and I are right in the middle of a meeting. Book tour business, you know."

"Oh, sure. I understand completely. All those logistics and schedules to figure out. Tracking all those book sales, figuring out how to spend all that hard earned money." She giggled.

"I'm so glad you understand."

"Maybe later then?"

"I'm afraid that we have to get back on the road soon. We have to be in Oregon by Wednesday."

Disappointed, she clutched her book. "I understand. Well, perhaps another time."

"I'd like that. It was nice to meet you, Josie."

Casper waved goodbye and closed the door.

" 'May all your dreams be hot and sweet?' "

"I suppose you could do better?"

"Shit, give me three months with a monkey and a typewriter, you bet I could."

10

*E*ight days later, with three more signings down, Either pulled the Winnebago into a rest area about fifty miles south of Portland. He and Casper stepped outside and sat at a picnic bench overlooking the Pacific and ate lunch.

"That friggin' thing is a bear to handle when the wind gets blowing," Either said.

"Yeah. It wears you out."

Casper took a bite of sandwich and stared out at the ocean. "Man, it's really pretty up here. I think I could live here."

Either glanced around the vast, undeveloped space. All the trees swaying back and forth in the wind. And green. He nodded. "Well, the nightlife would never kill you, that's for sure."

"Maybe I'll see if I can get a visiting professor gig in Eugene and teach writing."

"Shit," Either said. "You think some university is going to hire you to teach writing just because you sell some books?"

"I'm selling *a lot* of books," Casper said. "You know...I got to hand it you, the Winnebago idea was a stroke of genius."

"You're welcome," Either said, munching a handful of potato chips. "Nah, you'd probably need a PhD before a university would even talk to you. And you saw the way a couple of those professor wives started going after you last night at the signing. That's what you'd get working at a college."

"You'd think they'd have something better to do than come to one of my signings and start mouthing off during Q&A about how my books were...shit, I can't even remember the terms they used to describe them."

"They said your books suck. Doesn't matter what words they used. It was pretty hard to miss the point they were making."

"Other than that, it was a great crowd. Almost a hundred people. I thought the selection I used for my reading was a good choice."

Either chewed a mouthful of sandwich and stared at Casper.

"Blah, blah, blah…enough already, Professor. Why don't you talk about something important? Like the half million in diamonds we knocked off last night?"

"Yeah. Big night. We've already gotta be close to a million, maybe a million and a half."

"Probably."

"How long you want to ride this thing out?"

Either stared out at the ocean and followed a whale slowly making its way down the coast.

"Hello? I asked you a question."

"How long? Shit, I don't know. It's such a good gig. Since Amir's only gonna give us around thirty percent of what the stuff's worth, then we gotta split it. We still got a long way to go. But probably somewhere around the time we can both walk with at least a couple million."

"Is that all?"

"How much money do you need? Two million, tax-free, living on an island someplace warm and cheap."

"That's what you want to do? That's your long-term goal? Sit on your ass in the sand?"

"Sure. What's wrong with that? Buy a little place near the beach and find somebody nice to keep me company."

Casper, chewing while staring out at the ocean, considered the idea. "Not bad I guess. Maybe get a dog?"

Either raised an eyebrow and Casper laughed.

"Sorry. Forgot. Maybe get yourself a cat."

"A cat? If I'm already living with a girl, why the hell would I get a cat?"

"Once again, you lost me."

"Cats and women. Distant relatives of the same species."

"I'm gonna need a little more, Either."

Either put his sandwich down, placed both elbows on the table and leaned forward.

"You know how they say men are like dogs?"

"Yeah, sure. I've heard people say that. I'm not sure I agree with it though."

"Well, I've never been close enough long enough to any dog to make that comparison, but I have been around enough cats and women to see some similarities."

Casper took another bite of sandwich. "This oughta be good. Go ahead, enlighten me."

Either scratched the side of his head then cracked his neck. "Women are a lot like cats. And women, like cats, can be real independent. Plus they're both smart, and usually well-groomed."

Casper .

"But, they tend to be fickle. One minute you're hearing a contented purr, the next they're off chasing some sock you left lying on the floor."

Casper gave Either a blank stare.

"What?" Either said. "That's funny."

"And you wonder why you have problems with women."

"No sense of humor," Either said.

"Yeah, that must be it," Casper said. "You should be writing all these down."

"If there's one thing I won't be doing during our current business adventure is writing any of it down. And I'd strongly encourage you to do the same."

"I've been thinking about maybe branching out into crime novels. And you have to admit, this would make one hell of a good crime mystery."

"Only if the bad guys win."

Either picked up his sandwich and resumed eating, watching the whale continue to work its way south.

"So you're gonna stick with the writing after we wrap this thing up."

"Sure. Look at all the momentum I'm starting to build."

"So you want be a big star?"

"Sure. Why not? Romance books are big business and I like the genre. People feel good when they're reading uplifting stories about love. It gives them hope."

"I think they can be pretty schlocky."

"Sure. Some of them are. But I write great books. And you've seen me work a crowd, how I get and hold their attention. Yeah, why not? I certainly have the talent for it."

Either shook his head, then grabbed a napkin and wiped his mouth.

"Keep it up, Professor, and your head is gonna be bigger than your picture on the side of that Winnebago."

"Man, you're in a mood all of a sudden." Casper zipped his jacket and leaned back on the bench.

"Nah, that ain't it," Either said, voice barely above a whisper. "I'm really not…well, maybe. I guess it's a mood of some sort. But not like the kind you're probably thinking. It's not like I'm pissed off or anything. It's just that sometimes when I find myself in a place like this, so big…there's probably a better word for it than that but-"

"Vast."

Either scowled across the table then his eyes drifted back to the whale.

"Sure, whatever you say. Vast. So when I find myself surrounded by all this space, all green and beautiful with the ocean right there, I just start to feel…insignificant. I guess I shouldn't be surprised that everybody wants to be something else, huh?"

"Insignificant is a pretty strong term."

Either refocused on Casper.

"You watch any of those TV shows where there's some sort of competition? You know, singing, dancing, anything like that."

"I never miss *American Idol*."

"Perfect. Let me ask you a question. Who won last year?"

Casper sat quietly for several seconds, deep in thought.

"Shit. That's funny. I don't remember."

"But last year, when they were getting close to the end, you probably knew all the finalists, tried to figure out what songs they were gonna sing, what they were gonna wear and, knowing you, how you could get your hands on the phone number of the cute blonde singing all the country songs."

Casper thought for a moment, then shook his head.

"I don't think they had a blonde doing country last year."

"I'm just making a point. The whole time you were watching, it was so damn *important*, wasn't it? Six months later, you can't even remember who won. And I damn well know you can't remember who finished fifth two years ago."

"Who'd remember that?"

"Nobody would, Professor. That's my point. It's all about Flavor of the Month. And it's *temporary*, Professor, and another cautionary tale. Out of maybe a couple hundred thousand people trying out, somebody who's really talented manages to finish fifth and nobody remembers. Nobody fucking cares."

"I'm sure his family cared."

Either shook his head. "Here we go."

"You know I'm right. You're alone. That makes it all too easy for you to get inside your head and stay there. It's not healthy."

"You're something else, Professor. Next to me, you're the best jewelry thief I've ever seen. And I've met a lot of them. But for you, just like most other people, it ain't enough. All because you don't have a bunch of people cheering you on or telling you how wonderful you are. Not that I'm recommending thieves like us should go out and build a fan club."

Casper chuckled. "I just can't see myself doing this much longer. It's a young man's game. Plus, it might be nice to see what life on the normal side is like."

"You think driving back and forth to work an hour each way every day to a job you hate, plus all the other shit that goes with it, is normal?"

"Well, it seems to be working for a lot of people."

"Cautionary tales, my friend. Trust me, solo has a lot going for it." He nodded out towards the ocean. "Take a look at that whale out there."

Casper followed Either's stare and watched the whale's powerful yet seemingly effortless movements.

"What about him?"

"He's all alone out there. Just taking his time, enjoying the water. You think he gives a shit whether people like you and me are watching him swim?"

"How do you know he's alone? Or that he hasn't got a family?"

"I might not be the sharpest tool in the shed, Professor, but if there was another whale out there with him, I think I'd have seen him by now."

"Maybe he's going to work," Casper said, grinning at Either. "With a really long commute."

Either flashed that smile then turned serious again. "Trust me on this one, Professor. Normal is highly overrated."

"I'll take my chances."

"Not while I'm around you won't. Don't be taking any chances until we wrap up our mutual interests. Going back inside the joint isn't something I'd recommend. Or plan on doing."

"I don't see that happening."

"Nobody ever does, Professor." Either collected their lunch trash and dropped it into a nearby bin. "Time to hit the road. You're on later tonight and you need to shower and get cleaned up."

"What's the name of the town?"

"Shit. What is it? I can't remember. Cooch...coochie...cooze? Landing...? No, Bay."

"Coos Bay?"

"That's it. Gotta love the name. There's a nice little independent bookstore right next door to a family-owned jewelry store."

"Sweet."

"And there's an Indian casino right down the road from there. Maybe we'll swing by and play some blackjack later."

"Feeling lucky, huh?"

"Luck has nothing to do with. Your turn to drive. I'm gonna take a nap."

11

*E*ither glanced out the window of the Winnebago.

Several gawkers wandered around the parking lot, staring at the paint job, holding books, nudging each other; doing all sorts of goofy fan shit. Casper, wearing a towel around his waist and another draped across his shoulders, grabbed a beer from the refrigerator. He put it back as soon as he caught Either's glare.

"Why do you have such a problem remembering one simple rule, Professor?"

"Sorry. I forgot."

"No booze until after the job. How many times I gotta remind you? You're already starting to get sloppy. You losing your focus and concentration skills?"

"I said I was sorry. Just let it go."

Either sat down and pulled a folded sheet of paper from his pocket.

"Sit," he said, pointing at the chair directly across from him.

"I'm not a fucking dog."

"Lucky for you."

Casper shook his head, but stayed silent as he slid into the chair and started toweling his hair.

"Okay," Either said. "Final run through. You replace all the batteries in the flashlights?"

"Yeah."

"Get the fresh box of gloves?"

"Yup."

"Refill my acetylene torch?"

"That was on your list."

Either beamed.

"Just checking to make sure you're paying attention. You tighten all the bolts on the portable ladder? The other night it seemed like something was a bit loose."

Knowing they couldn't count on the luck of a small stepladder in every jewelry store they hit, they'd purchased a metal fire escape ladder they could roll up and carry.

"Yeah," Casper said. "It's fine. You just aren't any good on it. Swaying back and forth all the time."

Either studied the list.

"You get a chance to check out the external cameras?"

"Yeah. We could do it in our sleep. They've only got eight of them for the whole building. And there's none within twenty feet of the backdoor to the bookstore."

"Just inviting us in, huh?"

"Pretty much."

"What's the security system look like?"

"No problem at all. It's identical to the setup we had to deal with in Portland the other night. It's like the owners went shopping together."

"They continue to amaze and delight. Okay, I think we're ready. All right, Professor, get dressed and let's go see how many housewives end up wanting to get you in the backseat of their Volvo."

Fifteen minutes later, as they headed towards the bookstore's entrance, Either glanced at Casper's head.

"What did you do to your hair?"

Casper gently touched the side of his head. "Freshly coiffed."

"Freshly what?"

"Coiffed. Hair that's styled in an elaborate manner."

"Uh-huh," Either said, continuing to stare at Casper's hair. "Got it."

"You like it?"

"No, not particularly."

Inside the store they were met by the manager, a woman in her fifties who simultaneously gushed at Casper and ignored

Either. She tugged Casper's arm and led him to the back area of the store, where he'd be doing the signing.

Either glanced around then wandered past a section called Classics: big scary books that looked serious, books supposed to make you look smarter just by buying them and sticking them on your shelves. He headed for the magazine section, scanned the skin mags, selected one of his favorites, then reconsidered. Probably not a good idea for the business manager of a romance writer to be seen flipping through *Swank*. This looked like a classy bookstore, and Either was pretty sure they probably had a different definition of swank from the guys who published the magazine. He put it back and stood by the racks, flipping through the latest issue of *Playboy*.

"I hear there are some good articles in that issue."

Either turned around to put a face to that voice.

He'd been surprised many times in the past. Like the time he'd gone into the master bedroom of a house outside Atlanta, thinking it was empty, when he heard a woman's voice from under the covers say, 'Is that you, George? Be a dear and get me another Ambien from the bathroom. And a Xanax too.' Either, staying cool the whole time, left the lights off and retrieved the pills. She washed them down with water, saying, 'Thanks, baby,' then went back to sleep.

Surprised?

Sure. Shit like that really got your attention. Made you sit up and take notice.

Like the time he approached a hot Asian chick who talked to him with a southern accent, tossing around y'all like she'd invented it, smiled and listened quietly while he ran through his lines, eventually saying 'I'm real sorry to tell y'all this, sweetie, but you won't be getting any sugar from this girl.' Telling him to fuck off, but being real nice about it.

Yeah, things like that could surprise you, maybe even take your breath away.

But seeing her for the first time was different. This was like that commercial where the girl is driving down the road not

74

paying attention to what she's doing, fiddling with the radio, texting to her buddies, just having a great time when – BAM – she runs a red light and gets crushed by a truck going fifty. It was over. Just like that.

That's what seeing her for the first time reminded him of.

Either took a couple of deep breaths, recovered, and beamed at her.

"Articles? I wouldn't know. I'm more into...photography."

"I bet you are."

Either continued to smile as he checked her out. Gorgeous face, even though it seemed she was doing her best librarian impression to hide it. Long hair tied back in a ponytail, showing off the longest neck he'd ever seen. A bunch of small diamond earrings running up and down one of her ears. Wearing baggy chinos and an even baggier sweater, hiding all the good stuff. But Either was betting that underneath all that cotton and wool she was built, maybe even stacked. This was one to get to know, he decided. And judging by the intense stare she was giving him, like she was trying to see inside, this was one to look out for.

"Can I help you find something?"

What a voice...smooth, like velvet. A voice you'd enjoy listening to no matter what ball busting message she was handing out.

"You work here?"

"I do. Actually, I just started last week. I was working at another bookstore down the road, but it closed. Books are a tough business these days."

"Tell me about it," Either said, returning the magazine to the rack. "I deal with it every day."

"Really?"

Sounding to Either like she was saying *'you're fucking kidding me, right?'*

"You know the guy who's doing a signing tonight?"

"Casper something or other? Writes those dreadful romance novels."

Either beamed. Beautiful and smart.

"That's him. Well, I'm his business manager."

"Really?"

Again with the 'You're fucking kidding me, right?' She might be gorgeous, with a voice that could melt butter, but she was starting to piss him off.

"We're on tour at the moment. Giving him the chance to meet and greet with all his fans."

"Yeah, I heard all about it. The Endless Book Tour. If he didn't write that sort of crap, it would probably be a good adventure to be on. Well, at least your bus looks comfortable."

"It's a Winnebago."

"Thanks for clarifying."

Man, the attitude on her. A combination of 'Get over here and get yourself some of this' and 'What the fuck do you think you're doing? Go away.'

Tough to pull off.

Even tougher to deal with.

"So, you're into adventure, are you?"

"Sure. Can't you tell? What with me working in a bookstore and all. I got it all here. Adventure. Mystery. Science fiction. Self-help."

"Self-help." Either flashed that smile. "That reminds me. You hear the one about the woman who wrote a book on masturbation she thought would be a bestselling sex book but it ended up a total failure?"

"Because all the bookstores put it in their *Do It Yourself* section?"

"Oh, you heard that one."

"A couple times, yeah."

Either took a deep breath and then took his shot. "Look, if you aren't doing anything later on, maybe we could get together for a drink somewhere."

She continued to smile. "Sorry, but I'm busy tonight."

"Boyfriend?"

"Not this week. But hopefully it won't be long." She studied Either's face as he continued to beam at her. "What?"

"Your voice," he said. "It makes even a *no* sound good."

She smiled and glanced towards the back of the bookstore.

"Well, I need to go help set up for your friend's signing." She extended her hand. "I'm Coco by the way."

"Nice to meet you, Coco. I'm Either. Either Ore."

"Either or what?"

"Either or fucking nothing. Either Ore. That's O. R. E."

"Unusual name."

"Well, I'm an unusual guy."

"So I can see."

She smiled and walked away leaving Either wondering what the hell she meant by that.

**

"And then she said, 'So I can see.' What do you think she meant by that?"

"Probably demonstrating that she's a really good judge of character. C'mon, move your ass. It's late, I'm tired, and lugging this ladder is a total pain in the ass."

"Yeah, well it sure beats trying to lift you up by one arm through the ceiling."

They made their way back along the crawlspace towards the bookstore. Either stopped again.

"Did you get a good look at her?"

"Didn't get a chance. I spent all night trying to keep a safe distance between me and the manager."

"Yeah, the woman was in heat."

"Dragged me back into her office and stuck her tongue down my throat."

"Any good?"

"Tell the truth, I was too busy sneaking looks around the office trying to get the lay of the land to pay close attention."

Casper adjusted his backpack. "But, yeah, I guess she was a good kisser. Definitely eager. I'll give her that much."

Either nodded, then resumed his hunched shuffle along the crawlspace.

"But this, Coco. Man, I tell you. There's something special about that girl."

"Well, they say it's the quiet ones you have to watch out for," Casper said, adjusting his backpack again.

"That's the thing," Either said. "She's not really quiet. But she ain't loud either. She's got something going on inside that head that you just can't put your finger on."

"I doubt if that's where you wanted to put your finger."

"You got that right. I'd kill for a shot at that. But you know what I mean, right? I tell you that one is special."

"Too bad we're leaving Oregon," Casper said, brushing a cobweb away from his face.

"Yeah. Too bad."

"Did you at least get her number?"

"Shit. I forgot."

"Dumbass." He then reached out and grabbed Either's arm. "Hold up," Casper whispered.

"What?" Either stopped and turned to face Casper.

"Did you leave the office light on?"

"What? The office in the bookstore? How stupid do you think I am?"

"Are you *sure*?"

"Professor, someday I swear I'm gonna smack you in the head."

"Shhh. Well, just slide down there and take a look."

Either inched his way slowly along the crawlspace, saw the beam of light, then looked back at Casper and nodded.

"Goddamn it, Either."

"Hey, fuck you," he whispered. "If I say I didn't leave the light on, I didn't leave it on. Got it?"

"Well, somebody did. Shit."

Casper gently removed his backpack, pulled out his Glock, and checked the magazine.

"Man, I hate guns."

He waited until Either had done the same, then nodded for him to approach the open ceiling. Either peered down into the office, saw nothing unusual, then stuck his head further through the open ceiling panel. Seconds later, something large and heavy smashed against his shoulder and deflected off the side of his head. He dropped the gun as he rolled, semi-conscious, off the side of the desk. Casper glanced down into the office, but hung back out of sight on the crawlspace directly above the office. He extended the Glock and tried to see what was happening down below.

"Motherfucker," Either said, grasping his shoulder, checking the side of his head for blood. He waited for his vision to clear, then saw the Glock lying a few feet away.

"Go ahead. Reach for it. I dare you."

Man, she really did have the voice of an angel. He glanced up from the floor, used his arms to push himself up, and came to a sitting position. Staring hard at him was Coco holding a softball bat and ready for the next pitch.

"Hey," Either said, "do us a favor and put the bat down, okay?"

She moved Either's Glock closer with her foot, then picked it up and tossed the bat into the far corner of the office.

"Hey, you, Romance Guy," she called up to the ceiling. "Drop whatever you're carrying and slide your ass down here, nice and slow."

"You a cop?" Either said, staring in disbelief.

"What do you think?"

"I'm gonna go with no, but that just might be wishful thinking on my part."

She laughed but continued to stare up at the ceiling. Casper's hand holding the Glock appeared and the gun dropped to the floor. She retrieved it and slid it into her Chino's. She waited as Casper stepped onto the ladder and climbed down.

"Sit on the floor next to Maybe."

"It's Either."

"Whatever. Just do it."

"What the fuck are you doing here?" Either said, massaging his shoulder.

"Isn't that the question I should be asking you?"

"I guess. If you want get to technical about it," Either said.

She laughed, relaxed a bit, and sat down behind the desk. "What a pair of screw-ups."

"We have our moments," Casper said. He watched Either rub his shoulder.

The girl waggled the gun at him and said, "I thought you'd be out somewhere, giving Mrs. Williams a private reading."

"Who?"

"Sylvia. The women who spent all night drooling on you."

"Oh, right. Her. Not really my type. She's a real piece of work."

"She's just a scared woman trying to hang on while the business she spent twenty years building dries up."

"I imagine it's tough watching that happen to one of your friends," Either said, continuing to work on his shoulder.

"I just met her last week," she said. "I'm sympathetic, but she's not a friend. She's more of a life lesson. A cautionary tale so to speak."

Either stopped rubbing his shoulder and looked at Casper. "I told you there was something special about her."

She glanced at the ladder under the open ceiling panel, letting it all play out, putting it all together. "There's a jewelry store next door." She glanced back up at the ceiling. "So that's what this whole thing is about? A book tour where you peddle that romance crap, then come back later and knock off jewelry stores?"

"Hey," Casper said. "It's not crap. I don't understand why so many people feel the need to belittle the genre simply because it's a commercial success."

She smiled and shook her head.

"That's not why I don't like romance novels."

"Probably just another literary snob," Casper said.

Either frowned. "Shut up, Professor. Rule number one, never argue with someone holding a Glock on you. Especially one who doesn't like your books." Either glanced up at her and flashed that smile. "Yeah, that's pretty much it. You're a quick study."

She nodded and smiled. "Unbelievable. Actually, when you think about it, it's fucking brilliant."

"Thank you," Either said. "It was my idea."

"Good for you. I'll make sure to point that out during my testimony. *You'll* probably end up getting an extra ten years."

"Shit," Either said. "If we go up for this, another ten years ain't gonna make a bit of difference."

"What the hell are you doing here?" Casper said. "It's after midnight."

"I was working, idiot. I told Whatever earlier when he asked me out that I was busy tonight."

"You asked her out?"

"Hey, I took a shot. I mean, shit, look at her. She's gorgeous."

"Aren't you sweet," she said. "But too dumb to follow up with another question like 'Oh, you're busy. What will you be doing?' You were too worried about finding out if I had a boyfriend." She glanced around the office. "Say, where's your stuff?"

Casper nodded up at the ceiling. "Couple of backpacks up in the crawlspace."

"Go get them. And don't do anything stupid. Just climb up, drop them on the floor then get your ass back down here."

Casper nodded and climbed back up the ladder. Moments later, the backpacks landed. He climbed down and sat back down next to Either, still working on his shoulder. She placed them on the desk.

"Let's say we take a look at how lucrative this book tour is."

She searched the backpacks, found the two zippered bags, and dumped them out on the desk. She stared down for several seconds, then back at both of them sitting on the floor like two school kids in timeout.

"Holy shit," she said. "All this is from tonight?"

Either and Casper glanced at each other and nodded in unison.

"Wow. Impressive. Nice work, guys."

"Thanks," Either said. "You know, you don't sound anything like a librarian."

"I'm not a librarian," she said. "I work in a bookstore."

"You know what I mean," Either said. "How you managing to stay so cool, given the circumstances?"

She shrugged. "It's probably mostly genetic. My dad was a cop and my mother has ice water running through her veins."

"She sounds nice," Either said.

She stared at Either. "You really have a hard time keeping your mouth shut, don't you?"

"Hey, no need to get personal," Either said. "I was just commenting on something you said about your mom."

"No, she's not a mom. She's Mother. The well-known and richly deserving author of *50 Shades of Bitch*."

"I haven't read that one yet," Either said.

She stared at him in disbelief, looked at Casper, who shrugged his shoulders as if to say 'See what I have to deal with?' then laughed. She toyed with the diamonds scattered across the desktop. She caught Casper and Either staring at each other. "Let's try not to forget I'm holding a gun that could turn both of you into sausage okay?"

"I can live with that," Either said.

"So you never read romance?" Casper said.

"You mean the kind of crap you write? Not a chance. Give me an Elmore Leonard or James Ellroy and I'm happy. I read shit like yours and I get a stomach ache."

"You don't read anything other than crime novels?" Casper said. "Doesn't that give you kind of a limited perspective?"

"Probably," she said, "But I don't care. The whole world is a fucking toilet, so I figure I might as well learn as much as I can about why. And I don't think my perspective is hurt very much by not subjecting myself to four hundred pages of drivel about a jockey who falls off his horse and spends the rest of his life looking for love from the comfort of his wheelchair."

"What are you talking about?" Either said.

"*Shorty Rides Alone*," Casper said. "One of my earlier books. Not my best work."

She snorted then tossed her ponytail back behind her head. "Actually, my long-term goal is to write crime fiction."

"Sweet Jesus," Either said. "Not another one."

"So where are we at here?" Casper said, glancing around the office.

"Good question, Romance guy. I was just wondering that myself. On the one hand, I could just pick up that phone and call the cops. Keep the gun on you until they get here and probably get a nice reward, get my picture in the paper, maybe even win Citizen of the Year."

"Or?" Casper said staring hard into her eyes.

"Or I could just walk out of here with both of these bags. Take off to someplace warm and just kick back. I doubt if either one of you would be interested in turning me in, given everything you've been up too."

Casper nodded, then looked at Either who was deep in thought. Either looked first at Casper, then at the long-necked girl pointing his Glock at him.

"Or," Either said.

"Or what?" she said.

"The Professor and I could just add a partner."

"Really?"

But this time she didn't say it like, '*You're fucking kidding me, right?*' This time she was saying, '*Tell me more.*'

12

*T*he conversation, if a screaming match in the front seat of a car between two guys with a woman in the back seat holding a Glock could actually be called a conversation, was informative. And highly entertaining. Funny how one day, one chance meeting could make you reassess and adjust your plans, maybe even accelerate them. And if one was looking for adventure, and she was, this could end up being one hell of a ride.

The short version of the argument that had started quietly but quickly turned heated went something like this:

Either, the supposed brains behind the operation – and wasn't that a scary thought - had begun by asking, then repeating the same question, 'Why not?' Not taking 'Because I said so' as an adequate response, Either shifted gears and tried appealing to the Professor's testosterone level. 'Just look at her. She's gorgeous.' Unmoved, the Professor smiled at her through the mirror and nodded. 'Yeah, she is. So what?' Either immediately went on point. 'So what? I'll tell you so what. Tell me you ain't interested in the possibility of waking up and seeing her first thing each morning?' 'Actually I'm more worried about the possibility of waking up and seeing some hairy guy named George first thing in the morning for the next twenty years.'

That's okay, guys, she'd said to herself. *Please continue. Just pretend I'm not even here.* Back and forth they went. In the space of ten minutes she'd heard herself referred to as gorgeous, hot, fuckin' hot, smokin', smokin' hot, fucking smokin', fucking smokin' hot, and, finally, a long-necked, long-legged, pillow-biting piece of cooze which Either felt the need to turn around in his seat and apologize for. She told him she appreciated the imagery and, confused, he turned back around and shifted gears again.

Either: Dangerous, but probably a lot of fun to be around if you could manage his anger. Smart and dumb at the same time. A bizarre combination but, on him, somehow it seemed to work. But that smile. Jesus, if he kept using that on her, he'd have her shorts off in no time. Not that she planned on sharing that tidbit with the idiot intent on giving her a close-up view of a pillow.

Back and forth they went. Punch, counter-punch, often below the belt. Relentless with each other, while debating the merits of cutting her into the deal. But at the same time, they seemed *comfortable* yelling at each other, calling each other Fuckwit and Dumbass. It was almost as if they both knew they weren't actually fighting, just simply getting to a decision that, in her mind, had already been made. An old married couple, she decided. That's what they reminded her of. But rather than arguing about whose turn it was to take out the garbage, they were fighting about how much longer they'd have to work to cover another partner's share and whether or not they'd have to worry about whether or not the fuckin' smokin' hot piece of cooze in the backseat would decide one night to just put a bullet in their heads.

Good question, Professor, she thought as she listened and smiled, nodding her head.

Casper: The perfect example of the kind of guy she found repellent, but never seemed to be able to say no to.

Fucker.

Self-absorbed, and completely full of shit. Yet with a goddamn confidence level that always put her off her game. Kept her from thinking straight. Always left her wondering 'What the hell does he know that I don't?' Ego and testosterone both off the charts and still climbing. And good-looking with just enough physical imperfections to make him come off as real and not some male model pushing cologne or styling gel. Although he could certainly handle that commercial. The guy used enough hair product to fill the women's room at a dance club. And he was a criminal. A real pro. Certainly a big step up from the third rate burglars and dealers she was used to. A *professional* jewel thief and, combined with his looks, a killer combination that was more than enough to get her horizontal. The only thing saving her was the fact that he wrote books she wouldn't even use as doorstops.

Shit, if this guy wrote crime fiction, she'd be toast.

Buttered on both sides.

Stay with the plan, girl, she told herself. Stay distant, aloof, maybe even a little mean if necessary. Don't let him in. You know what happened the last time.

By the time it was over, the argument seemed to have ended in a draw. But that was irrelevant. As long as she had the Glock, she was pretty sure she was getting on that Winnebago.

"It's funny," she said. "I've had this car for two years and this is the first time I've ever sat in the back seat."

Either draped an arm across the top of his seat in front and turned to look at her.

"You never had the chance to get back there with some guy, fool around a bit, get all hot and bothered?"

"Hot, no. But I'm starting to get the bothered thing working."

"Huh?"

Casper laughed without taking his eyes off the road. "Smooth."

"Well, I just thought, smoking hot as you are, you'd have had a lot of opportunities."

"I've had lots of chances to do that…Either." Better start using his name before he got pissy and started to pout. "But I've never *chosen* to do that."

"Shy, huh?"

"No. I'm just more of a hotel kind of girl."

"Sure," Either said, nodding. "I can see that." He turned back around in his seat and looked out the window.

"Dumbass," Casper said.

Moments later, Either turned back around.

"You know, I was just saying earlier to the Professor that this would make a good crime novel."

"What would?" she said, stretching out in the backseat.

"This thing. This entire adventure."

She considered the idea, then nodded.

"It probably would. But only if the bad guys win."

Either turned back around and looked at Casper.

"I told you she was special."

13

*E*ither handed Coco her third glass of wine and beamed at her. She smiled back, not even trying to match Either's wattage, and held her glass up in toast. Either took a sip of beer then stretched out on the convertible couch and studied her, but trying not to be obvious about it. Working on a nice midday Chardonnay buzz, hair pulled back in a single braid exposing that long neck, loose white men's dress shirt tied above her navel, and cutoff jean shorts that pretty much showed off all the good parts. A washcloth could do a better job covering her, he decided, not that he was complaining. She was wearing the pair of five hundred dollar sunglasses Either had grabbed for her during last night's job. Definitely not something a lot of women could afford to wear, but not unique enough to draw attention. She stared out the window as they worked their way down the coast. Coco relaxed, occasionally throwing out some remark about how beautiful and green it was, what a nice day it was, general small talk shit that he and Casper would try to outdo each other agreeing with.

Either watched her as she studied the Professor behind the wheel, doing his usual slow-poke driving. So far, she hadn't seemed to show a preference for either one of them over the other. But she wasn't showing any real interest in either of them. He was torn about that one; he'd be disappointed if he never got a shot at her, but if she ever hooked up with the Professor, he'd be downright pissed. Better that both of them miss out than have him get there.

He watched the Professor tapping his fingers on the steering wheel to some crappy southern rock. Bastard. The guy had everything going for him. And why? Because he wrote shit down that made women cry and twitch? How hard could that be? Either wasn't sure about how to handle the twitch part, but he was pretty sure he wouldn't have any problem making women cry. He'd pretty much been doing that for years.

Coco arched her back, and her shirt pulled tight across her chest. Either couldn't stop staring even when she caught him. He blushed and forced a smile. She shook her head and giggled, gulped her wine, and asked for another. Either refilled her glass and stretched back out on the couch.

"Tell me about your books," she said, turning in her seat to face Casper.

Casper glanced over. "What do you mean?"

"Your books, you know. What are they about?"

"Yes, Casper," Either said. "Please tell us all about them. *" Maybe the moron will expose himself for the idiot he is.*

Casper puffed up in his chair, then started in. "Well, let's see. First of all, I write books about love. About people faced with choices…choices between good and evil, love and hate…those looking for the good in other people, or those" - glancing back at Either - "finding fault at every turn." He gave Either a 'take that' smile, then looked at Coco and flashed her one that said, 'See what a sensitive guy I am? How about you and I get horizontal?'

"Interesting," she said. "On the surface it would seem they could be written off as sentimental trash."

Either beamed. *Go get him, girl. Tear him a new one.*

"Yes," Casper said, taking time to get his response right. "I suppose that's possible, if people don't take the time required to examine the different layers at work in my books. What appear to be traditional romance stories with a little extra bit of heat thrown in," – he flashed her a coy smile, - "have a vast tapestry at work underneath the main narrative. It's like unpeeling the layers of an onion."

"Onions," Either said. "So that's how you make them cry. Who knew?"

Coco snorted, spilling some of her wine in the process. Either one.

Fuckwit zero.

Casper ignored Either's commentary and continued. "But most of all I write about people trying to find happiness amid a sea of life's challenges. Redemptive, uplifting, timeless…those are the things I write about."

"And throbbing manhood," Either said.

"It's a metaphor," Casper said, glaring at Either through the rearview mirror.

"You know," Coco said, "I have noticed you do tend to use it a lot."

Casper deflated in his seat. "You really think so?"

"But what do I know?" she said, reaching out to touch his arm. "You're the writer."

"Yeah, he's a real stud-muffin when it comes to the *sexual* metaphor," Either said, feeling buzzed.

"I suppose you could do better?" Casper said, still eyeing him through the mirror.

"Easy. Piece of cake."

"Hah. You think it's easy to write a good sex scene?"

Either shrugged. "How hard could it be?"

"Hard enough to be throbbing," Coco said.

She and Either burst out laughing.

Casper fumed and tightened his grip on the steering wheel.

"This could be fun," she said, regaining her composure. "Let's do it."

"Write a sex scene?" Either said.

"Sure. Why not?"

"Well, I know I'm *up* for it. If you get my drift."

She stared at Either through narrowed eyes.

"Really, Either?"

"Sorry. Okay, how do we get started?"

"Let's see," she said. "I'll start with a word or a phrase, and we'll just take turns building on it."

"Sounds great. Hey, maybe you'll get something you can use, Professor."

"Highly doubtful," Casper said, staring down the highway.

"Okay, what do we need to get started…hmmm…I guess we'll need a pair of panties in the scene," Coco said.

"What the fuck we need panties for?" Either said. "We're writing a sex scene here. Wouldn't they just get in the way?"

"Hey, it's my turn and if I want to use a pair of panties, that's what we're gonna do," Coco said, her voice raised, sounding angry. But she had to be faking it. At least that's what Either hoped. "A pair of panties. Now it's your turn."

"Okay, panties. I guess we'll need a color. How about red? Red panties."

"Nah, not red," she said. "Too many color variations."

"Hey, it's my turn. A second ago, you tell me to mind my own business when you just had to have a pair of panties in the scene. So how come you get to criticize and change what I want to do?"

"Because I'm a girl, Either."

Casper laughed and grabbed his water bottle. "Yeah, you two are gonna write a sex scene."

Coco glared at Casper, then refocused on Either. "Pick another color."

"Okay, okay. Let's see what color of panties is she wearing…how about lavender?"

"Perfect. Lavender. I love it. Okay, she's wearing lavender panties. What kind? Let's see. How about scant?"

"What the fuck is scant?"

"Barely adequate."

"Well, if they're barely fucking adequate, what do we need with them in the first place?"

"Humor me, Either."

"Told you it wasn't easy," Casper said.

"All right, my turn," Either said. "Let's see…we got a pair of barely fucking adequate lavender panties…"

"Scant."

"Sure. Whatever you say. A pair of scant lavender panties covering her…what?" Either sipped his beer, deep in thought.

"Hah. Told you."

"Shut up and let me think. Okay, how's this? A pair of scant lavender panties covering her nether region."

"Nether region?" Coco said. "A place of darkness or eternal suffering? Sorry, Either, but that's not gonna work."

"That's what nether region means? Huh, who knew?" Either stared off into the distance. "I thought it meant pussy."

"Don't be vulgar, Either."

"What's wrong with pussy?"

"There's nothing wrong with it but we're writing a scene for a romance novel, not a letter to Penthouse Forum."

Casper laughed again. "His throbbing manhood approached her nether region…you guys are on a roll. It sounds like something out of a Star Trek episode."

"Captain, I can't hold it much longer," Either said.

They both laughed until they caught Coco's glare.

"Can we refocus here?"

"Sorry," Either said.

"Okay, we need some action in the scene," Coco said. "Give me a good action verb."

"Action, huh? Okay…stimulated."

"Nah, too obvious."

"Probed?"

"Too clinical."

"Implemented?"

"Too corporate."

"Illuminated."

"Illuminated? What, they're doing it in the dark?"

"Well, how the fuck do I know? Maybe they're shy."

"C'mon, Either. Think."

"You this demanding in the sack?"

"What?"

"You. In the sack. Demanding. Controlling all the action."

"Wouldn't you like to know?" she said, smiling at him over the top of her wineglass.

"Well, sure," Either said. "Who wouldn't?"

"Would that help?"

"What?"

"If you were imagining *me* in those barely fucking adequate panties."

Either shrugged.

"Probably couldn't hurt."

"Okay. Imagine I'm lying in the bedroom back there with nothing on except a pair of my scant lavenders. What would you do?"

"Well, I sure wouldn't be sitting around playing word games."

"So what would you do? Tell me exactly what you'd do."

"Well, assuming we've gotten all the preliminaries out of the way…you know what I mean?"

"I'm afraid to ask."

"Preliminaries. You know. Kissing and shit like that until I've covered all the usual suspects. And you've probably done a little bobbin' for apples."

"Bobbing for apples?"

"Yeah, you know what I'm referring to, right?"

"Sadly, yes, I'm sure I do. Okay, the preliminaries are over and I'm ready. What would you do?"

"Let's see. I'd pull…no…slide…no…I'd rip…ah, fuck it, truth be told, I'd probably tear them off with my teeth to get at you."

"Interesting choice. Then what?"

"I'd mount…no, I'd pound away with…what? High energy."

"You can do better than that."

"I'd pound away with…oomph."

"Oomph? I'd never sleep with anybody who used the word *oomph*."

"I'll remember that. Let's see…what would I do?"

"C'mon, Either. Let's go. I'm cooling off here."

"Okay, I'd pound away with…verve."

"Verve? Who the hell fucks with verve?"

"Well, if he fucks anything like he writes, probably the Professor."

Coco burst out laughing.

"Verve you," Casper said through the mirror.

"That's funny," Coco said. "But stay with me, Either. You're pounding away with what?"

"I'm pounding away with my throb-"

Casper snorted. "Told you."

"I'm pounding away with…gusto. Yeah, I'm gonna go with gusto."

Coco shrugged. "Well, it wouldn't be my first choice. But let's go with that. You're pounding away with gusto. Now what?"

"You want more?"

"Of course I want more. You're pounding away with gusto until…"

"Until you're…writhing."

"I'm way past writhing by this point, Either. Pay attention."

"Sorry. Okay, I'm pounding away and we're…sweating. We're dripping sweat."

"Dripping? Really? Yuck."

"Don't like dripping, huh? How about…shimmering? We're shimmering with sweat."

"Ooh. Nice alliteration."

"Nice what?"

"Never mind. Keep going. You're pounding away, we're shimmering with sweat until…"

"Until? Well…until I pop."

"Pop?"

"Yeah, you know, when I…pop."

"Yes, I know what you mean, but aren't you forgetting something?"

Either paused, deep in thought, and sipped his beer.

"What am I forgetting?"

"Me, Either. You're forgetting about me."

"Oh yeah. Sorry. I always have trouble with that part. Okay, let's see. I've chewed my way through your scant lavenders, pounding away, shimmering with sweat until you…explode. No. Quiver? No…I keep pounding away until you shudder."

"Good one," she said. "I like that. Until I shudder like what?"

Either closed his eyes and concentrated.

"Until you shudder like a Porsche with bad brakes going from eighty to zero."

"Well, it's a vivid image. I have to give you that."

"Thanks. I stole a Porsche one time that had really shitty brakes. It just kinda came to me."

Casper stared through the mirror. "Dumbass."

"Whew," Either said. "I need a cigarette."

Either lit one and shared the pack.

They drove the next twenty minutes smoking in silence.

14

*E*ither and Casper leaned against the back wall of the
bookstore, both doing their best to not stare at their new partner,
who was chatting with the manager. Dressed casually but still
stylish, with tight jeans and a lavender silk blouse Either figured
she'd chosen just to torment him. He wondered what color
panties she was wearing and whether they were barely fucking
adequate. Her hair cascaded down her back tonight, swaying
and flowing as she nodded, laughed at something the manager
said and touched his arm, then brushed some imaginary muffin
crumb off his cheek. Either admired the way she was handling
him, but had to admit to a touch of jealousy.

"Just look at her working him over," Either said. "The guy
won't know what hit him."

"Yeah." Casper took his eyes off her long enough to give a
fan a casual wave, then refocused on Coco, now taking the
guy's hand and giving it a squeeze. "She's a total pro."

"Still regret cutting her in?"

"I'm…torn," Casper said. "But I'm dealing with it."

"A hundred bucks she lets him give her a tour of the
storeroom in the next two minutes."

"You're on. She's gonna tell him she'd love to see it, but
wants to wait until later when the crowd thins out and they can
have some private time to themselves. Give him some time to
think about it, check her out some more as she wanders around
the store."

"She's good," Either said, continuing to watch Coco work
the manager.

"Yeah," Casper said, nodding and sliding into smarmy as
another fan walked by. "It's so nice to see you. Thanks for

96

coming." Casper took a sip of coffee and refocused on Coco. "The classic femme fatale."

"French, right?"

He glanced at Casper, who nodded.

"Deadly woman."

"Shit, let's hope not."

"I can certainly think of worse ways to go," Casper said.

They watched her draw the manager close, whisper in his ear, peck his cheek. She walked away slowly, knowing full well he was watching every step she took.

Casper tossed his coffee cup in the trash and checked his reflection in the window.

"You owe me a hundred bucks."

They both smiled at her as she approached. She glanced back and forth between them with a puzzled expression.

"What?" she said. "Did I miss something?"

"Nah," Either said. "We were just talking."

"About me?"

"You see anybody else in this store worth talking about?" Either said, tossing his empty cup into the trash.

"You're so sweet." She flashed a quick smile, then turned all business. "I'm going to get a personal tour later on. What are you going to need?"

"General description of the storeroom and office layout so we know where we're going, where the light switches are, ceiling type, where they keep the ladder with wheels – what a great invention that was – let's see, anything else, Either?"

"Password to the back door would be nice."

"Yeah," Casper said. "But that might be tricky. If you can get him talking about himself, showing you some of his favorite memorabilia, shit like that, he might let something slip or have it written down somewhere. But if you can't, don't worry about it."

"I'll get it," she said. Again, she saw both of them beaming at her. "What is wrong with you two?"

"Nothing," Either said. "We're just…impressed."

"I haven't done anything yet. Save it for later. I'll do a card trick. Maybe beat you at your favorite game."

"Or maybe a little…bobbing for apples?"

"Why? Am I talking too much?"

Casper laughed. "Classic noir."

Either stared blankly at both of them.

"You'll have to excuse him, Coco," Casper said. "He's pretty good at the big picture, but sometimes whiffs on the details. Before you came over, he said you reminded him of one of the femme fatales from the classic noir period."

"Either said that?"

"Well, he had a little help," Casper said.

"I'm going to take that as a compliment, Either," she said, touching his arm.

"Hey, I agreed with him," Casper said.

"Yeah, but I said it first."

Coco's expression brightened. "I love the women in those roles. Self-sufficient, smart-"

"Sexy as hell," Either said.

"Of course," she said. "Smoldering sexuality was central to their role. You know, it's interesting. If you study the films of that period, they were constructed in ways that made sure the *femme fatale*, independent as she was, had to lose. And the lead male character, despite whatever temptations and dalliances he fell prey to, in the end, it was central to the narrative that he remained dominant and reaffirmed male control."

"Fascinating construct," Casper said.

Either, who'd lost the plot right around the time he'd heard her say *femme fatale* in that voice, stared at her.

"So you're saying…?"

"I'm saying that it was okay for him to pursue, even get horizontal with the bad girl, Either, but he couldn't end up living happily ever after with her."

"Why not?"

"Because it was fucking Hollywood." She paused when she saw his puppy dog face. "I'm sorry, Either."

98

"You don't have to yell at me."

"I'm sorry. I tend to get worked up when I start talking about this topic." She lowered her voice. "Let me try again. What did your grandmother do, Either?"

"My grandmother? What do you think she did? She was a grandmother."

"Before she became a grandmother."

Either considered the question. "Well, I know she was a mother too, but I'm pretty sure you're not referring to that. During world war two she worked in a factory."

"Perfect. And did she keep working there after the war ended?"

"Nah. She stayed home, pumped out a bunch of kids."

"There you go. There's a theory that the noir films were part of a misogynistic…" She glanced at Either.

"Yeah, misogynistic. Go on. I heard you," he said.

Coco glanced at Casper, who shrugged.

"Hey," Either said. "You get called something often enough, eventually you're gonna grab a dictionary and look it up."

She smiled at him and continued. "So anyway, there's this theory that the noir genre was part of a misogynistic construct to help try to reshape traditional societal roles after the war ended. You get my point?"

"Yeah, you're saying that women had to work during the war to help make sure we didn't lose everything to the Japs and Germans, but when it was all over, the government and businessmen who called all the shots wanted them back in the kitchen where they thought they belonged."

"Outstanding, Either. Very good."

"Can you say that again without making it sound like I'm some kid riding the short bus who just learned to tie his shoes?"

"Sorry."

"It sounds to me," Either said, "like the women in those movies were actually the initial women's libbers. It's just that no one, including them probably, knew it at the time."

"Wow." Coco nodded, glanced at Casper, then back at Either. "Outstanding."

"That's better," Either said, nodding, the determined grimace now replaced by that smile.

Satisfied she'd gotten him back, she continued. "You know the novelists of that era, the ones that wrote pulp crime, had a lot more freedom. They could be more creative, and their storylines often challenged existing stereotypes."

"Ones where the bad girl wins?" Either said.

"Exactly." She shook her head. "Shit, now you got me saying it." She refocused. "They could use twists and turns that Hollywood would never have accepted in those days. And they wrote some great strong female characters that were incredibly sexual, yet still worthy of respect, even admiration."

"True," Casper said, nodding, rubbing his chin.

Coco watched Casper's attempt to play sage but avoided comment. "But, of course, some of the women turned out to be absolute monsters," she said, smiling back and forth at them. "It's just nice to sometimes read something that surprises the hell you out of you." She glanced at Casper. "Something where you don't know the ending by the time you get to page twenty."

"Hey. Are you saying my books are predictable?"

Either laughed. "Who's slow now?" He looked at Coco. "Man, you know a lot about this stuff."

"I may be a criminal, Either, but I can do other things." She glanced around the bookstore. "Okay, I think it's time for our little *noir* operation to get to work."

"I like that," Either said, "Noir operation."

"It's incomplete," Casper said.

"What do you mean?" she said.

"Well, we have our femme fatale, and Either makes a great cynical malcontent. The disaffected, living on the edge, burnout."

"Hey," Either said.

"But we don't have the all-American sweetheart. Eager, yet virginal. Cute, but content to remain blissfully unaware of everything going on," Casper said.

"Ah, don't sell yourself short, sweetie," she said, patting Casper's cheek. "That's what we've got you for."

15

*E*ither waited for the signing to start. He debated between being able to spend the next hour ogling Coco standing off to one side behind the Professor but having to endure him droning through another mind numbing reading, or heading to the front of the store for another cup of coffee and some peace and quiet. It had been too long since he'd had the chance to just sit and think, try to get a handle on where they were at, where this thing was headed.

Plus, the coffee was really good.

He heard the Professor clear his throat and read the first sentence. That was enough to drive Either towards Starbucks.

The Professor's selection this evening was a chapter from the new one he'd been working on the past week, while ruining the Winnebago's *ambience*, as the Professor liked to call it. Either was driving, trying to chat with Coco, with the Professor constantly interrupting the flow with 'Yes, that works' and 'There simply has to be a better way to say that' or even cutting them off mid-conversation to read a paragraph out loud, then ask for their opinion. Shit. Guy was just rude and so full of himself. But sneaky. Either knew, behind him saying he 'just needed to get some work in' the real reason was that he was trying to use his advantage with words to impress her, doing everything he could to keep Either from having time to weave a little magic of his own on her. Either acted normal, just putting his real self out there, see if he got a nibble.

So far; nothing, just talking to him in that voice, smiling and laughing, even occasionally reaching out to touch his arm. Yeah, that was the way to go, he decided. Just be yourself, let it play out. Like she said, they were still only in the second act, whatever the hell that meant. Let the Professor, wanker that he was, keep trying to come off like he was Shakespeare or Will Rogers with a bad case of Tourette's.

Either paid for his coffee and sat down at a table.

"I see roach season has come early this year."

Either looked up, took a moment to place the face, then beamed at the man.

"Well, I'll be. Agent Roberts. And look at you. Carrying a book. How about that? FBI guy with a book. Crazy world we live in, huh? Whatcha reading? Cop novel about some action hero packing serious heat, saving the world, giving you a big woody?"

"How you doing, Either?"

"Can't complain, Agent Roberts. You?"

"I've been better." He sat down, set the book on the table, and glanced around the bookstore.

"Are you actually reading that?" Either said, recognizing the cover. "I wouldn't have figured you for a romance guy."

"It's for the wife," he said. "I saw in the paper he was doing a signing here tonight, so I thought what the hell. She's a big fan of his."

"Aren't they all," Either whispered. "Hey, I thought you were divorced."

"A guy can't buy a present for his ex-wife?"

"Free country. Think that's gonna be enough for her to let you slide back between the sheets once in a while? You know, give you the occasional one for old-times' sake."

"Highly doubtful."

Either thought about it, then nodded. "Yeah, imagine it would be." Either pointed at his coffee. "Want one?"

"No. I'm meeting some buddies at a bar down the street in a couple of minutes."

"What the hell you doing all way up here in California?"

"Vacation."

"Bullshit."

"Why not? Maybe I'm heading off to a tour of the wineries."

"Yeah, and maybe I'm gonna be stomping the grapes. You don't take vacations, Agent Roberts. You're always on the clock."

"Okay. Let's just call it an extended break."

"Now you're talking." Either grinned and lowered his voice. "Who'd you beat the shit out of this time?"

Agent Roberts grinned as he reached across the table and took a sip of Either's coffee. "Just another scumbag I should have had the good sense to walk away from." He slid the cup back. "It's good. Not sure it's worth four bucks a cup."

"Price of progress, Agent Roberts." Either picked the cup with his fingertips, reached behind him, and tossed the cup into the trash. "So you went out and kicked the shit out of somebody else for a change, huh?"

"Yeah. But if it's any consolation, Either, I was thinking of you the whole time."

Either laughed and flashed that smile.

"I know how tough handling anger can be. But I'm working on it. I tend to suffer from the same problem, but I doubt it's as serious as yours."

"No, probably not. Your pathology manifests itself in different ways."

"Well, look at you. Reading books and using big words in a sentence. You must be coming up for a promotion. Or you probably were before you rearranged that guy's face. How long did you get?"

"Two months. Without pay."

"Shit. I do that to somebody in a bar, no matter how good my reason, you'd lock me up for a couple of years."

"If you only got two, Either, I'd consider myself a failure."

"Shit. Why sit around wait to draw that conclusion, Agent Roberts? A lot of us have been thinking that about you for years."

Either glanced around and focused on a wall at the far end of the bookstore.

"You know, Agent Roberts, I always wondered something."

"What's that, Either?"

"Does the Bureau recruit assholes who enjoy kicking the shit out of people, or is that part of the training program?"

"Probably a little bit of both. What are you doing here, Either?"

"I'm working."

"Yeah, that's what I thought. I saw the jewelry store next door."

"No, Agent Roberts, you got it all wrong. No more of that life for me. I've gone legit. I'm just one more working stiff these days."

"Bullshit."

"You know, Agent Roberts, given your tenuous relationship with the Bureau, I'm sure they would just love to hear that you're up here hassling the shit out of somebody who's doing nothing other than sitting here trying to enjoy a quiet cup of coffee. Which you managed to fucking ruin a couple minutes ago."

Roberts leaned back in his chair and studied him.

"Tenuous relationship? What you'd do, Either? Join some Word of the Day club?"

"I just told you. I'm reformed. Chosen a new path."

"Sure you have." He laughed. "So what's the job?"

"I'm a business manager."

Roberts laughed louder. "Of what?"

"Not of what." Either nodded at Casper who was speaking to the assembled crowd, waving his arms, touching his hair to make sure it was still in place. "Him."

"You're his *business* manager?"

"Yup."

"Now you're just fucking with me, aren't you?"

"Although that is one of life's greatest pleasures, Agent Roberts, in this case I'm not. I put this whole tour thing together, and I'm pleased to say that we are doing very, very well."

"Really?"

The way he said it reminding him of Coco. Either beamed at him and nodded. Roberts turned in his chair to look at Casper, then looked back at Either in disbelief.

"Really?"

"You already said that. I heard you the first time."

"Son of a bitch."

"I'm a changed man, Agent Roberts."

"Who's the woman?"

"Her? That's his new agent. She's gonna take care of stuff like foreign sales, movie and TV rights. You know, handle all the shit I don't know much about."

"Big job."

"Fuck you."

"Be careful, Either. I'm still an FBI agent."

"And I'm just a regular citizen minding my own business. We clear on that?"

Agent Roberts stared at Either, who continued to flash that smile at him.

"Yeah. For now." He stood and picked up his book.

"Nice seeing you, Agent Roberts. And thanks for buying a book. We appreciate it."

Roberts smiled. "Yeah, my pleasure." He glanced back at Coco. "She's hot. You getting anywhere with her, or has the writer snapped her up?"

Either's smile disappeared momentarily, but returned.

"A little personal, don't you think?"

"Everything you do, Either, is personal with me."

"Well, let's try to maintain at least a little mystery, huh?"

"Sure. Let's save something for later. But let me ask you one more question before I go."

"Knock yourself out, Agent Roberts."

"If he's got a quality piece of trim like her around, what the hell does he need you for?"

Either closed his eyes, took a moment to focus on his breathing, and then looked up.

"You take care of yourself, Agent Roberts. Hope to see you again sometime real soon."

"Oh, I'll be around, Either. You can count on that. In fact, I plan on being there at the very end to hear your final request."

"Something like, Agent Roberts, please put that fucking gun down?"

"Exactly."

16

*E*ither was stretched out on one of the convertible couches, enjoying one of the rare occasions when the Professor didn't have all the answers. No relaxing and getting comfy for the Professor right now; he was pacing, wearing out the carpet. Coco was in the kitchen cooking dinner-not the *galley* as the Professor kept calling it-making some pasta with shrimp dish that sounded good. Cooking, she said, not because she was succumbing to some expected female role, surrendering to an outdated society norm, no, cooking just because she felt like doing something nice for the two of them. Sure, the Professor had said; *that and fact that's it your fucking turn.*

Things had gotten real quiet for a while after that.

The Professor was still pacing, making Either tired just watching him. Smoking and pacing, pissed off because he wasn't writing, couldn't write because he couldn't concentrate. There was too much on his mind now that the FBI had got his attention, and he blamed Either since it somehow just had to be all his fault. Like he somehow had control over what Agent Roberts did and whose life he decided to make miserable.

"Jesus, Either," he said, lighting another cigarette. "What did he say he's doing here?"

"Just relax. Shit. He said he's visiting friends while he's on suspension."

"And you believe him?"

"Fuck no."

"Then what is he doing?"

"You're gonna give yourself an ulcer, Professor. You know, I got some good relaxation techniques I could show you. Help you chill, refocus all that nervous energy."

Either beamed at him, received a cold stare then shrugged.

"Hey, he's just doing what FBI guys do," Either said. "Sniffing around, getting in your face, doing his *my dick's bigger than yours* act. Don't worry about it."

Casper stopped pacing, sat down and tried to make eye contact with Coco. Failing, he looked at Either.

"So what's he want with you?"

Either shrugged. "We have history."

"You want to talk about it?"

Either shrugged again and stared out the window. "Not really."

"Of course not," Casper said. "A very selfish perspective if you ask me."

Either stared hard at Casper who shook his head and crushed his cigarette out. He waved wafting smoke away from his face and folded his arms across his chest.

"Tell me one more time exactly what he said."

"Jesus, Professor. You're worse than a three-year-old."

Coco snorted, but listened closely.

Casper, worn out, lowered his voice and looked at him.

"Humor me. Just tell me what he said, Either."

Either stared at Casper and deadpanned, "He said he thought your stuff was a watered down rip off of Nicholas Sparks' early work."

"That fucker. What would he know?"

Coco laughed and nodded at Either, who beamed at Casper.

"Fine. Laugh all you want. But this is not good." He got up and resumed pacing. "I think we need to cancel tonight's job." He ran his hand through his hair, deep in thought.

"What?" Either said, sitting up.

"You said yourself that he made reference to a couple of recent robberies up the coast."

"So what? Look, Professor, I know this guy. Trust me, he's just fishing."

"And he knows you. That's a problem. No, I say we cancel tonight. Besides, we could all use a night off. Let's just kick back, maybe catch a movie."

"No," Coco said, placing two steaming bowls of pasta on the table. "Let's just stick with our plan."

"That's easy for you to say," Casper said, sitting down and spreading a napkin across his lap. "It's not your pert little ass that's on the line here."

"Ah, that's so sweet. But the quality of my ass, and whether or not it's on the line here, is not really the point," she said, sitting down with her own bowl and starting to eat. "This is good, if I say so myself."

Either mumbled agreement through a mouthful of food. Casper took a bite and chewed, staring off into the distance.

"Let's at least discuss our options," Coco said.

"No way," Casper said.

"Let's hear her out," Either said.

"Thank you, Either. At least there's one gentleman on this bus." She fiddled with her noodles, picked up a shrimp with her fingers, and chewed as she glared at Casper.

Either looked back and forth between his two partners. Definitely some history bubbling up to the surface. Too hungry to worry about why she was so pissed off, he slurped down a mouthful of noodles.

Coco ran a fork through her noodles then set it down, wiped her mouth, and took a gulp of wine.

"So if this FBI guy-"

"Agent Roberts."

"Yes, thank you, Either."

She flashed him a dark look, glaring just long enough to make him uncomfortable. Damn, Either thought, kicking himself under the table.

"If Agent Roberts is already trying to link us with those other jobs and we don't go in tonight, that might make him even more suspicious. He obviously knows there's a jewelry store right next door."

"But if we do go in tonight," Casper said, "won't that just be giving him one more reason to start looking at us even harder?"

"Not if we lay it off on somebody else," she said, taking another gulp of wine, staring off into space. "Yeah, that's it. We just need to find someone to take the hit."

"You mean like a patsy?" Either said.

"Patsy? What, now we're back in the 1940's?" Casper shook his head as he toyed with his food.

"Hey, it was just a suggestion. I don't give a shit what we call it." Either looked at Coco. "What's another term for it?"

"Dumbass comes to mind," she said, glaring at Casper.

"Jesus, will you fucking let it go?" Casper said, glaring right back at her, their eyes locked.

Either watched the dance of the scorpions. He had to give the Professor credit. The man could turn up the hostility when he needed to, and he tried to hang tough. But her…shit, when she got pissed off, she had a tendency to stay there, right in the zone, working it to perfection.

"We just need to redirect Agent Roberts' hard-on for Either. Come up with a little misdirection. Give him someone else to focus on."

"Find some sucker to manipulate," Either said, liking the idea a lot, silently considering the possibilities.

"Yes."

"By tonight?" Casper said.

"Sure," Coco said, staring out the window, wheels continuing to turn.

"How the hell are we going to do that?" Casper said, slurping noodles, getting some all over his shirt.

"I guess that's my problem, isn't it?" Coco said, glancing at the mess Casper was making. "You eat like a pig." She got up and put her bowl in the sink. She turned and looked back at Casper. "And it's your turn to do the fucking dishes." She sat down at the table and glanced back and forth at both of them, elbows on the table, arms folded. "Just how easy can the two of you make it?"

"Make what?" Either said.

"The whole thing," she said. "Disabling all the alarm systems, video feed, getting into the safe, then getting out without leaving any traces."

Either looked at Casper. They shrugged in unison.

"Shit," Either said, "We make it look any easier, everybody's gonna want to start trying it."

"But who needs all that competition, right?" Casper said.

Both men laughed. Coco let the laughter play out and die down, then continued.

"Would it be possible for you to disable everything? You know, be completely ready to go in, but just hang around for a while?"

"Hang around?" Casper said. "Jesus Christ, Coco. It's not like we're taking a fucking trip to the mall."

"Could you do it?"

"Of course I can do it. But that's not the point."

"You don't even know what the goddamned point is yet," Coco said, eyes flaring again. "Look, just go in like you always do, but stay up in the crawlspace right above the jewelry store and just wait there."

"And do what?" Casper said.

"Bring a book to read," Coco said. "But not one of yours. We need you awake."

"Hah," Either said. "Now that's funny," he said, turning to Casper. "Because it's true."

Casper ignored them. "And just how long are we supposed to hang out up there?"

"Until I call you, of course," she said, now smiling at both of them. She stood and rubbed her neck. "Let's see. I need to change, then I'll need to get back into town. We passed a restaurant on the way in. I can just walk up there and call a cab."

"A cab to where?" Casper said.

"Well, I don't know that yet, do I? But I'll find it. Every town's got one."

She headed off to the bedroom. Either and Casper, clueless, went back to their dinner. When they finished, Casper did the dishes, while Either, sprawled on the couch, watched an episode of *House Hunters*.

A half hour later, she emerged as a hot Goth dressed in leather with purple hair, black lips, emerald eyes, and a red snake tattoo on one side of her neck. She twirled in her fuck-me pumps and smiled.

"What do you think?"

"I wouldn't recognize you if I bumped into you on the street," Casper said.

"That's kinda the point," she said, doing a half-turn. "Either?"

"Makes me want to go over to the dark side."

"You're already on the dark side, Either."

"Not that fucking dark."

She laughed and headed to the door.

"Just make sure you're ready to go by midnight. And remember to put your phones on vibrate."

She closed the door behind her.

Casper grabbed a dish towel and started wiping down the table.

"I don't like not knowing what's going inside her head," Casper said. "Don't like it at all."

"Well, one thing we do know is that she's pissed at you."

"Yeah."

"Wanna talk about it?"

"Not really," Casper said, tossing the towel in the sink. "But she worries me sometimes."

"We're just going to have to trust her. That she knows what she's doing."

"Yeah, I guess," Casper said, checking his hair in the mirror. "But just to be safe, I'm gonna pack an extra clip for the Glock."

17

*C*oco stepped inside and waited until her eyes adjusted to the light. One thing about cab drivers, she reminded herself, was the good ones always knew what you were looking for. And where to take you to find it. She'd climbed in the back seat, flirted just long enough to get his attention, and then asked him to take her to the biggest shithole they had in town. You know, she said through a thin Goth smile, that one special place in town where a girl like her could pretty much find anything she was looking for.

The guy had nodded at her through the mirror, then offered to show her the perfect place, his place. If it was a real shithole she was looking for.

She looked around the bar: Dark, dreary, and depressing. Just like its clientele.

She nodded at the thick-necked bouncer, already ogling her as she walked past, headed to the bar and sat down trying to remember if Goths drank anything special. She ordered a beer, keeping it simple for the tattooed thug working his way slowly up and down the bar at his own pace.

Beer in hand, she swung around in her stool to face the room, ready for work. Eager, feeling like she finally had something tangible to do, a purpose for being here, making a real contribution to the *team*, as the Professor insisted on calling them.

Dumbass.

She tapped the beer bottle and nodded. Before she was done with this thing, he was gonna pay for that one.

Working her way through the first beer, she thought about them. Finally past the playful flirting, playing word games. Now way beyond her being just their traveling companion, like some dancing bear with an attitude and great tits. They were always playing one-up with each other, seeing which one could impress her, make her laugh. Not that she minded. She liked both of them and, who knew, maybe she'd end up giving Either a shot at her before they were done.

But not the Professor.

Cross him off the list.

The fucker.

Up to this point the situation had been okay, something new and different to do, but, lately, she'd gotten bored. Sure, she could keep playing the cockteaser, could play that role in her sleep. But tonight it would have a bigger purpose than just using it for fun on those two, practicing her skills, staying sharp for a moment just like this.

Cockteaser extraordinaire.

Yeah, that was her.

But she had so much more to offer.

One by one they approached the bar only to be, dispatched with a small smile or, when necessary, a gruff 'fuck off', combined with a glance at the bouncer more than happy to play Sir Galahad for her if necessary. All the men, plus two biker chicks with high hopes approached, laid it out for her consideration, then skulked off, determined to get the buzz back she'd managed to kill with just a wave of her hand.

She ordered another beer and hoped this wouldn't take too long. One thing darkness couldn't hide was the smell. She finally spotted what she was looking for at the end of the bar, caught his eye and flashed a hint of a smile. It was always tough playing Goth; needing to come across as a total nihilist, yet still showing just the right amount of girl.

The guy at the end of the bar ordered two beers, had one delivered to her, then slithered in her direction. She watched him approach. Petty thief or small time dealer, she decided.

Hopefully both.

Definitely a dealer, she decided as he got closer. And one who looked like he used a lot more than he sold. Going for confident, almost managed to pull it off, but ended up coming across as stupid and wired. On meth, she hoped. Crank heads had the perfect combination of pseudo-courage and unpredictability she was looking for.

"How ya doin?"

"Getting better, now that you're here."

She forced a smile at the balding guy with two long stringy braids trailing down his back. His head looked like an egg with rope handles. The rest of him was all bones and nervous tics.

"Buy you a drink? Mebbe get you something a little stronger? A little pick-me-up to get your night going in the right direction."

He swayed, grabbed the bar to steady himself, and sat down next to her.

"You just bought me a drink."

He stared at her, but seemed to be looking off into the distance. "That's right. I forgot. Mebbe get you something a little stronger. A little pick-me-up to get your night going in the right direction."

"How sweet. Repetition. I don't hear that used much. That usually work for you?"

"Huh?"

"Nothing. Just the beer is fine. I'm just trying to wind down a bit. It's been a bad day."

"I hear that."

"How come I've never seen you in here before?"

"Me? Here? I'm a regular."

"Really?"

"But I just got back in town."

"Business or pleasure?"

"Hey, if it ain't pleasur…ubble, what's the point of doing business, right? You know what I'm talking about?"

"Yes, I certainly do."

"Exactly." He drained half his beer, then looked at her. "What were we talking about?"

"You were just about to tell me where you've been while I've been sitting here all by my lonesome."

"I was up the coast."

"Oh. Northern California? Oregon?"

"Sure. California. Oregon. Couple of other states I can never remember the name of."

"Interesting. I hear it's beautiful up there."

"Sure. I guess."

"So what's your gig?"

"Ah, I do a little lab work," he said, grinning at her over the top of his beer bottle. "You know. I'm kinda a partner in a couple of small labs up there. Basically, I guess you could say I'm a product rep."

"Oh, I see," she said, grinning back at him. "Pharmaceutical sales."

He nodded, which proved to be too much movement. He swayed, grabbed the bar for support and stared, trying to focus on the backlit bottles lined up in rows on glass shelves behind the bar.

"Pharmaceutical sales. I gotta try to remember that."

"Well," Coco said, placing her hand on his forearm and realized she could touch her finger and thumb together. "As I was saying, my day was a joke. A total waste of oxygen."

"Why don't you tell me all about it?"

So she did.

About how she'd gotten fired from her shitty job, just because she got caught in the middle of a situation that simply wasn't her fucking fault. Her asshole boss hitting on her all the time, his wife noticing and her not being happy about some weird Goth chick working there in the first place. Besides, it wasn't like they had anything serious going on. It was just that one time. On his desk in the office, she said, giving Egghead a wink and placing her hand back on his forearm.

"You're a real mink, aren't you?"

"Minx."

"Huh?"

"Not important."

Then continued: What was wrong with that? She wanted to know. Just a one-time casual hookup, people like her and Egghead did it all the time, right? She gave him a moment to think about it, then plowed ahead, talking faster now. His eyes rolled back in his head from the sheer onslaught of words, his head dropping as he tried to keep up, take it all in. How the wife would have never known, but the dumb bastard just had to tell her, at first bragging, then getting mad back at her, trying to punish the wife by taking her to the office and showing her the exact spot on the desk, this big antique thing with claw-feet and pearl inlays. It wasn't very comfortable, but it was real nice.

"The fuck?"

"The desk. Pay attention."

The wife going ballistic, telling her she's 'fucking fired', those exact words right there in front of a bunch of customers, can you believe that shit? A *major* confrontation. She starts breaking shit, throwing stuff all around the office. Well, both of them can just kiss her tight little ass. A couple of ginormous assholes. Assholes that don't deserve to have all that money. And all those diamonds.

Coco paused, sipped her beer, and waited.

"Diamonds?"

"Yeah. Didn't I mention that? They own a jewelry store."

"Really?"

"Yeah, dumb bitch ended up breaking their security system." She laughed, fiddled with her hair, taking her time, getting ready to set the hook. "Their security system is on the fritz and they couldn't get anybody to come out and fix it until tomorrow."

"So you're sayin…" Trying so hard to focus.

She grabbed his arm, made sure she had what was left of his undivided attention, and lowered her voice to a whisper. "All I'm saying is that there's a whole store full of diamonds and gold, just ten minutes away from here sitting there unprotected for the next ten hours."

118

"Huh? You don't say."

"Yeah. You know, it would be so easy to…"

"To what?"

"Nothing. Never mind. It's crazy."

"Now you're speaking my language."

"Forget it."

"No, let's talk…I think I'm getting an idea here," he said, nodding. "Yeah, it's definitely an idea."

She squeezed his arm and whispered in his ear. "I could get in there real easy and the safe is really old, but I don't know anything about how to get into one of them."

"Anybody ever tell you that you got a nice voice?"

"Maybe once or twice."

"Real relaxing."

"That's so sweet. But let's try to focus here."

"Sure." He glanced at her. "What were we talking about?"

"Safes."

"Oh, that. No problem. I got lots of experience with them."

"That's good news, right?"

"Sure. I guess. So what are you saying?"

"What I'm saying is that I've got half a mind to go out there right now and do some major fucking damage."

He grinned. "And I've got half a mind to join you."

"You know," she said. "That might just be enough."

"Fuckin' Ay."

"You got a car?"

"Sure."

"That's great. You should probably let me drive."

**

"Casper, I'm bored."

"Read your book."

"Reading by flashlight gives me a headache. What time is it anyway?"

"Two minutes since the last time you asked me," Casper said. The guy had the patience of a dog waiting on dinner. "She's late."

"Relax, she'll be here."

"Yeah, and probably with your friend, Agent Roberts, in tow."

"Stop it."

"You know what would happen if they ever got a warrant to search the Winnebago and found our stash?"

"They'd never find it," Either said. "Even with a warrant."

"You with the secret compartment behind the fridge."

"It's brilliant and you know it."

"Yeah, it's pretty good," Casper said, nodding.

"And we're the only two who know about it, so let's keep it that way, got it?"

"Who am I gonna tell?"

"Nobody. You ain't telling nobody. Including her, got it?"

"Yeah. I got it." Casper sighed. "You know, I'm really worried about what might happen to my writing career if we ever got caught."

"Your writing career? We get caught with what's hidden behind the fridge, the only thing you'll be writing is letters to the governor begging for mercy."

"Man, I'm keyed up," Casper said.

"Yeah, me too," Either said. "Usually we get the adrenaline pumping, then get in, get out. This is like sitting around the locker room waiting for the big game to start." Either sighed. "I'm bored."

"Read your fucking book."

Either's phone buzzed. He lowered the volume and punched the speaker button.

"Where are you?" he whispered.

"I'm right outside," Coco said. "I just dropped him off behind the store."

"Everything okay?" Casper said.

"It's fine," she said, still pissed at him. "Is he going to have any trouble getting in the back door?"

"Can he handle turning a door knob?" Casper said.

"Questionable. He's a little out of it."

"What's he on?" Either said.

"Let's see…half a dozen beers, couple shots of tequila, and probably about two grams of crank."

"Meth head?" Either said. "You brought a fucking meth head? Shit, I hate those assholes."

"Just relax, Either. It's not like you're taking him out to dinner. Besides, he's calmed down quite a bit the last few minutes."

"What did you do? Feel the need to do a little bobbing for -"

"Relax, Either," she said, her voice calm. "Trust me, it was nothing like that. I slipped him about a hundred milligrams of Ambien."

Either looked at Casper, who shrugged.

"Is that a lot?" Either said.

"About ten times the normal dose."

"Shit. That oughta make him pretty easy to handle."

"You won't have any problem with this guy. You know the type I'm talking about."

"Taking up space, wasting all that good oxygen."

She cackled into the phone. "Ah, Either, you always make me laugh. Okay, guys I'm out of here. I'm gonna stash his car somewhere nearby and take the rest of the night off."

"Where you going?" Either said.

"I don't know. Probably find myself a nice hotel for the night. Take a long hot shower, wash this color rinse out of my hair, maybe order room service."

Either remained silent.

"What's the matter, Either?"

"Nothing."

"Look, I just need a break tonight, okay?"

"From us, right?"

"Well, if you're going to force me to say it, yeah, a break from both of you. But don't read anything into it." She waited and got nothing. "Either?"

"What?"

"Focus on what you need to do the next half hour, okay?"

"Okay."

"That's better. Look, I'll just rent a car and catch up with you guys at the signing tomorrow. Good luck."

She disconnected and Either put his phone back in his pocket.

"I wonder where she's going."

"Who cares?"

"Think she's got a date?"

"Actually, Either, I think she just needs to get some good sleep to get her energy back so when she sees you tomorrow she can jump your bones on a full tank."

Either started to respond but stopped when they heard the clang of metal on metal. They listened, heard it again and looked at each other.

"What the hell is that?" Either said.

They pulled on their surgical gloves and removed the ceiling panel. Casper peered down into the store.

"Jesus Christ," Casper said. "Fucking guy is going to wake up the whole neighborhood."

Either attached the collapsible ladder and let it unroll. He stepped on and began his climb down with Casper following, both of them cringing at the incessant clanging.

"The guy's a total amateur," Either said.

"Tell me about it."

As soon as they were on the floor, they pulled ski masks over their heads and grimaced again at the noise, even louder down here. Casper pulled his Glock from his pocket and nodded. Either pulled his gun and followed Casper to the office. They stood in the doorway and stared in disbelief at the emaciated shirtless guy with braids holding a crowbar in one hand and a large hammer in the other, pounding on the safe. So far, the safe was winning the battle.

"Hey, Chicken Wing. Why don't you take a little break?" Either said, timing his question between clangs. "Yeah, over here behind you."

The guy wheeled, wild-eyed, still holding the hammer and crowbar. He swayed, almost lost his balance, then steadied himself. He stood panting, sweating profusely.

Casper laughed.

"Hey, look. He's shimmering."

"Fuck you." Either then focused on the guy. "Why don't you drop those things you're making all that racket with, Cowboy? People are trying to sleep."

"The fuck you doin' here?"

Casper looked at Either. "Not a bad question."

"Yeah, pretty good. You want to answer him?"

"No, you go right ahead," Casper said, gesturing.

"Thank you." Either took a step closer.

"Come any closer and this crowbar goes upside your head."

"Is that right?"

"Fuck you."

"That's just the crank talking, Cowboy. Why don't you just drop the tools and we'll get on with our business."

"Fuck you."

"Impertinent little prick, isn't he?" Casper said.

"Yeah, man's got a bad attitude."

"Maybe this will get his attention." Casper snapped the Glock's chamber. The guy continued to sway as he stared in the general direction of the sound. "He's out of it."

"Yeah," Either said, "he's not gonna last much longer."

"Think you're so tough? I guess we'll see about that, won't we? The six of you come barging in here. Well, I'll tell you. You're gonna need all six."

"Shit, maybe I should give this Ambien a shot," Casper said. "Six?"

123

"Just go with it," Either said. He pointed his gun and got the guy's last bit of focus. "Okay, Cowboy, one more time. Just put those tools on the floor and everything will be just fine."

"Hey, I'm working here. Fuck you." The guy started to turn back to the safe.

"You hit that fucking safe one more time, and I swear, I'll shoot you right in the nuts."

Chicken Wing considered the comment, let it sink in, then dropped the crowbar and hammer and turned around. He swayed back and forth and yawned. "Man, I'm wiped out."

"Sure, I understand." Either said. "Been a long day and it's late. Why don't you just sit down on that nice comfy carpet and take a little nap?"

The guy yawned, then nodded and curled up in a ball on the floor.

"There you go. Take a load off."

"Six guys. They needed six guys to take me down," he murmured into the carpet. Moments later, he was snoring softly into an expanding pool of drool.

"Still worried about our partner?"

Casper shook his head. "No, I have to hand it her. This is pretty slick." He focused. "Okay, let's go. A hundred bucks you can't get in less than five minutes."

Seven minutes later, they were packed and doing their final check to make sure nothing had been left behind. Either looked at the guy sleeping peacefully on the floor.

"Ah, meth heads. They always look like such little angels when they're sleeping."

Casper laughed, placed the torch in the guy's hand to create a good set of prints, then placed the torch next to him. Either glanced inside the empty safe and closed the door.

"I would love to hear the first conversation this guy has with the cops."

Casper laughed again, took one final look around the office, then followed Either up the ladder. He reset the alarm system and video feed while Either retrieved the ladder and put the ceiling tile back in place.

"You want to set off the alarm?" Either said.

"Nah," Casper said, pulling on his backpack. "He'll wake up at some point and set it off himself. Or he'll sleep through the night and be a nice surprise for the owners when they open up in the morning. Let's go. No time to dawdle."

"Dawdle?"

"Yeah, dawdle. To waste time, to move aimlessly."

"I know what it means. That's not my point."

"Well, excuse me. I was just trying to help."

"Just do me a favor. Don't do that."

"Fine. Jesus. We're a little grumpy tonight, huh?"

Either tightened his backpack, started to work his way down the crawlspace, then stopped.

"Geez, I hope she doesn't have a date. I mean, it's really none of my business, but I thought we were making a connection. Getting close to something good happening. You know, something of a horizontal nature."

Casper sighed.

"Let's go. You're dawdling."

18

*H*er mother had always told her that she'd end up kissing a lot of frogs before marrying one. And then she'd laugh between gulps of martini, pretty much straight vodka without any olives or little onions to get in the way, shaken over ice until it was frigid; the perfect cocktail for her mother given her frozen heart and marinated liver.

Her mother.

Laughing at her joke about frogs but really laughing at Coco. Gawky, a mouth full of metal, her body not grown into itself yet. Five years later, she'd bloomed into a knockout, capable of making conversation-stopping entrances when she felt like it.

Her mother.

Now pissed off every time she saw her daughter, what with Coco reminding her mother of a time when she had been young and beautiful, with her whole life in front of her. Started trying a different angle to mess with her head, calling her *unenlightened*, her word for fucking stupid, and kept yammering on about frogs.

Her mother.

Not one word about Prince Charming. Certainly nothing about Coco ever finding hers. Thanks for that, *Mother*.

Never a word about princes.

Just frogs.

Like the hairy troll lying on top of her at the moment, dripping sweat.

She'd checked in a little after midnight, cleaned up and changed, then went downstairs to the bar where she met up with him right before last call. He was hammered, a good thing since it gave her the perfect excuse to just climb into bed and get some sleep. But this morning, she'd been out of excuses.

The guy was definitely a pounder. And sweating up a storm. But given the hairy back, he sure wasn't shimmering. He was…what? *A sweaty pounder*. Perfect, she decided and giggled to herself, making a mental note to remember that one. Then she was brought back to the moment when the guy started whispering in her ear, calling her baby. And his bitch.

Bitch?

I'll have you know I'm the smokin' hot piece of cooze from the back seat. A smile flared as she remembered the moment; then it faded. She stared up at the ceiling wondering if the stench of scotch and cigarette smoke would be as hard to get out of her hair as that purple rinse had been. Grimacing now, fighting the onset of a leg cramp. She tried to reposition herself as the cramp built and spread to her foot.

The sweaty pounder noticed.

"Good, huh? I know what you like, right? I know this is the way you like it, baby." He grunted and picked up the pace. "Yeah, you're my little bitch, aren't you? I might just go all morning."

Fat chance that's gonna happen, Agent Roberts.

"Yeah. I'm gonna go all morning."

Time to pull out the big guns. She wrapped her legs around his waist and started whispering in his ear, kissing and nibbling his neck.

Three minutes later, she was in the shower with the water as hot as she could stand. She toweled off, tied the thick robe tight and headed back into the bedroom.

Agent Roberts was sitting up in bed, talking to somebody on the phone, speakerphone on so he could take notes. Coco sat down in a chair next to the bed and listened.

"Last night?" Agent Roberts said, confused.

"Yeah," the guy on the other end of the phone said. "We found him passed out inside the store with the torch he used to cut the safe right next to him. Had his prints all over it. Dumb fuck."

"He was probably on something."

"Gee, ya think, Agent Roberts?" The guy, obviously a cop, laughed. "I've always heard you FBI guys were pretty sharp."

"Funny guy," Agent Roberts said, jotting something down in his notebook.

"Well, whatever cocktail he was on must have been good. The guy is still rambling on about meeting up with some chick with purple hair and six guys in ski masks."

"Six?"

"Shit, the guy was so out of it, it could have been him hallucinating into a mirror."

"How'd they find him?"

"The alarm finally went off after he started waking up from his nap."

Agent Roberts lit a cigarette and offered one to Coco, who shook her head no.

"The store got a video system?"

"Yeah. We're looking at it now, but so far all we got is the guy snoring and drooling on the carpet. No signs of forced entry. Nothing. And the place was cleaned out."

"Hmmm," Agent Roberts said, blowing smoke up at the ceiling.

"Yeah, I know what you're thinking. Awful similar to the other ones up the coast."

"Any chance this guy has been up there recently?"

"Bingo. The guy just got back in town after spending the last three weeks up there, but he's having a hard time remembering exactly where he was. Imagine that."

"Son of a bitch."

"Yeah, I think this is the guy. And we certainly got him cold for last night."

"And you said that the torch has his prints all over it?"

"Sure does. He swears he's never seen it before. Actually said it couldn't be his because, get this, he's never used a torch in his life."

"Dumbass."

"Yeah, most of them are."

"If you like, I could bring my Rottweiler, Tank, over to encourage him to talk."

"Thanks," he said, laughing. "That might be fun to watch. But we figure he'll eventually try to shorten his visit with the state and give his partners up. For now, he's hanging tough. Swears he always works alone. What do I care? Guy wants to play the martyr, knock yourself out, right? I can close this one today and probably help the locals up the coast do the same."

"Okay. Thanks, Detective. Keep me posted if anything changes."

Agent Roberts ended the call and tossed the phone aside. He thought in silence for several moments, then looked at Coco.

"I told you," Coco said, pulling on her jeans.

"Doesn't mean he's clean. Look, baby, I know this guy."

"Well, so do I," Coco said. "You still got the dog? I remember him. He was just a puppy back then."

"Not anymore. He's ninety pounds of mean."

"Sure. Like father, like son."

"Funny girl. He's spoiled too. I just bought a special collar that monitors his vital signs. Sends the results to an app on my phone. Since I'm away from home so much, I feel better if I can keep an eye on how he's doing."

"You're such a humanitarian, Agent Roberts," Coco said, tired of the dog story. "Look, I'm telling you Either's not involved."

"Of course he's involved…he's involved in something. He's gotta be. Once a thief, always a thief."

"Why do you have such a hard-on for him?"

Agent Roberts patted the mattress. "Speaking of hard-ons. Why don't you come back to bed and I'll tell you all about it?"

Coco forced a smile and turned coy as she sat back down in the chair and buttoned her blouse. "No, we both know perfectly well what will happen if I do that. Just tell me the story. If it's a good one, maybe I'll get back in bed when you finish."

"Oh, it's a good one," he said, lighting another cigarette. "You remember the summer when we first met?"

"Kinda hard to forget the time in your life when you're forced to start working undercover for the FBI."

"Hey, you had a choice," Agent Roberts said.

"Sure, five years in prison. Some choice."

"It was still an option."

"Just tell the story."

"Okay, relax. I'd been assigned that summer to work undercover, trying to get inside a major dope operation that was operating out of L.A. I'd just started working for the Bureau and, since I'd grown up there, and-apart from my family-nobody knew I'd just joined the Feebs, they figured I'd be the perfect guy to work on it. You know, just some young kid working a shitty summer job, living at home with his Grandma, out partying, trying to get laid."

"How is your Grandma, by the way?"

"She's great. Ninety-two and going strong. Still plays bridge once a week with your mom. Well, when your mom's not travelling."

"Let not talk about my mother, okay?"

"You've always been too hard on her."

"She sold me out to the FBI. Fucking sold me out to you."

"It was for your own good." Agent Roberts finished his cigarette, then looked at her. "And it kept your ass out of jail."

Coco stared off into space. She'd been working a beautiful short sale mortgage scam when her mother had gone snooping in her room, probably looking for some coke to take the edge off the vodka, when she found all of Coco's paperwork. Couldn't believe what *her* daughter, *her* only child, had gotten herself mixed up in. Just had to confide in someone about it, and then, maybe, do some shopping with, but being sure to get back home in time for happy hour. Decided that his Grandma living down the street was the best choice, since the rest of her friends were simply *unenlightened*. Just like her daughter. Grandma, shocked, feeling sorry for her mother, could only think of one thing: tell my grandson the FBI agent. He'll know what to do.

Coco was sitting at her desk in the fake office she'd rented for the summer, holding a cashier's check for almost four hundred grand, ten minutes away from heading to the airport. There was a knock on the door, actually more of a thump, and there was Agent Roberts in the office, pointing his gun at her, but speaking in a soft voice, so *concerned* for her wellbeing. Laid out the terms of his proposal to her, but never shared them with anyone else, including the FBI or Grandma. Just told her that it was all a big misunderstanding and that he'd taken care of it. Grandma passed the good news on to her mother, who celebrated by getting hammered then screamed at Coco to get the fuck out of her house and not to come back.

So Coco ended up doing his dirty work for no money. Six years of infiltrating, uncovering, doing whatever it took to get the information Agent Roberts needed to close a case, advance his career.

Six, no, now almost six and a half years.

Should have taken the five years in prison.

"Penny for your thoughts?" Agent Roberts said, reaching for his pack of cigarettes.

"How about I just tell you to go fuck yourself and you get on with your story?"

He laughed and lit a cigarette.

"Anyway, that summer I was working undercover, three of the drug suspects played on the same softball team and, since I'd spent a lot of time playing ball, even played some in college...you know that, right?"

"No. But I always imagined you did spend a lot of time in college playing *with* your balls."

"Cute," he said, forcing a quick smile. "So they asked me to play on their team. I figured it was a great way to get closer, keep an eye on them."

"Yeah, I got it. Work, work, work. Continue."

"You'll never guess who else was on the team."

"Either."

Agent Roberts nodded. "Yup. Our old friend, Either Ore. Hey, good guess."

"Thanks. I'll take asshole FBI agents for a thousand, Alex."

He raised an eyebrow at her, but let the comment pass.

"Yeah, old Either played right field. He could hit and was fast as well, probably got that from making all those getaways, but couldn't field for shit. Fucker couldn't catch a cold. Cost us a couple of games."

"I thought you said this was a good story."

"I'm getting to it. Anyway, it didn't take us long to figure out Either spent a lot of time in second-stories. Guy never seemed to work but had a great car, really cool apartment up in Marina del Rey, right on the water, but still close to the airport. Gotta be sure about those getaways, right?" He turned on his side and propped himself up with an elbow. "At the time, I didn't give a shit about him. Some small time thief. Who cares? Besides I was working on something much bigger. And then it happened."

Finally, Coco thought. She pulled her legs up and folded them under her on the chair.

"What?"

"You know anything about precious stones?"

"A little. Like diamonds?"

"No, I'm talking about the really valuable stones. Rare ones you don't see very often."

"No. I wouldn't have a clue."

"Unenlightened," he said, smiling, just to fuck with her. "One night one of my Grandma's family heirlooms disappeared without a trace. Someone had gotten in her house, opened the safe, removed the heirloom, then closed the safe and…poof. Gone."

"What was it?"

"It's was a bracelet. A one-of-a-kind bracelet my great…no, great-great grandfather made. But from what I've heard from my Grandma, I'm not sure great is the term I'd use to describe him. He always sounded pretty fucking mediocre if you ask me. And mean. But the man loved to travel in search of precious stones. Travelled the world for twenty years and eventually came back home with a big bag of stones. Plus cirrhosis and a nasty case of syphilis."

"A real renaissance man."

"Exactly. The bracelet always made me think of that movie, *The Maltese Falcon*. You know, like if they had actually found a jewel-encrusted falcon, it would have been similar to the bracelet."

"It was a book."

"Really?"

"Yeah, classic noir. Dashiell Hammett. 1929."

"Well, who's got time to read? This bracelet was amazing. It had, let's see…Red Beryl he found up in Utah that goes for around ten, maybe fifteen thousand a carat. Alexandrite from Russia, supposed to be even more valuable. Jadeite and Painite from Burma."

"Myanmar."

"What?"

"The country. It's now called Myanmar."

"Well, it was fucking Burma when he was there, okay? I'm trying to tell a story here. Both of those rocks are really rare. Painite goes for around sixty thousand a carat. Let's see…what else? A bunch of diamonds he got who knows where. The bracelet had a couple dozen stones set into a huge chunk of gold."

"It sounds amazing. So you think Either stole it?"

"Of course he stole it. Who else? One night we were all sitting in a bar after a game, and we starting taking a few shots at Either, poking fun at him, telling him how his hitting and running skills were going to come in handy in prison, shit like that. Then we somehow gravitated to talking about jewelry and then, like the drunken idiot I was, I told them pretty much the same story I just told you."

"And then it got stolen?"

"Eight days later. To this day, my Grandma still blames me, never lets me forget that I was the one who broke the family heirloom tradition. Funny thing was that the bracelet was supposed to pass from her to me. A priceless, unique piece of jewelry worth more than most houses supposed to be handed down to me, but I'm the one who caused it to be stolen in the first place. You know what I call that?"

"Ironic."

"Ironic? Who gives a shit about irony? I call it a fucking tragedy."

"And you confronted him about it?"

"I did more than confront him."

"What did you do?"

"I beat the shit out of him." Agent Roberts crushed out his cigarette. "Almost killed him."

"So that's what this is all about?"

"Yeah. Strictly personal. I went up to him before the start of one of our games, asked him about it. He just kept denying it, looking at me with that annoying grin on his face. Then he got tired of me trying to push him around and told me to go fuck myself."

"I like his smile."

"Well, you oughta. His new one probably cost him around fifty grand."

"You knocked his teeth out?"

"Shit. That was the least of his problems. Getting hit with a softball bat a dozen times will do some serious damage."

"Jesus Christ."

"Amen. And pass the ventilator."

"What did they do to you?"

"Major suspension. Got pulled off the undercover work and spent a couple years trying to work my way back into the good graces of the Bureau."

"With my help."

"Yeah, I guess you played a part."

"You're such a prick."

"Again, my dear, Coco, this was your choice. You remember the day when I told you it was a better option for you to work undercover for me rather than spend five years locked up."

"You mean the day you said if I agreed to get horizontal with you, and keep doing it when you told me to, you'd keep my cute little ass out of prison?"

"Tomato, tomahto, baby. Besides, I don't ever remember hearing you complain about it before. Consider it a perk. One of the fringe benefits."

"Well, I'm tired of it," she said getting up out of her chair to look out the window. "I want out."

"We can talk about that sometime later. Hey, I almost forgot to ask you. How'd you ever talk your way into being that guy's agent?"

She shrugged, still looking out the window. "They're both in heat. I could have told them I was an axe murderer, wouldn't have made any difference."

"Thinking about finally coming to your senses and joining the family business?"

Coco turned to look at him and shook her head with a small smile.

"Not a chance. That's never going to happen."

"Too bad. Just think how rich you'd be."

"I'm already rich."

"Yeah, I imagine you are. You ever talk with your mom?"

"Not in six and a half years." She stared back out the window. "You think he still has it?"

"Who, Either? The bracelet?"

"Yeah."

"That would be my guess, but who knows. It's so unique, it would be almost impossible to fence. I guess you could take all the stones out and sell them individually, but I can't see Either doing that. The man's a total criminal, but he seems to appreciate the finer things in life. I think that, to him, breaking down that bracelet and selling it off in pieces would be…almost sacrilegious."

Coco nodded and then turned away from the window.

"What would you do if I was able to get it back?"

Agent Roberts snorted.

"Baby, if you were ever able to track that down and get it back to me, your days working for me would be over. "

"Promise?"

"You'd never hear from me again."

"What about Either?"

"What about him? I'd never be able to prove he took it in the first place. Actually, it's probably better for me and my career if I never see the guy again. He gives me that stupid grin one more time, I'll probably fucking shoot him."

"You'd look good in orange."

Agent Roberts chuckled and lit another cigarette.

"Never gonna happen. You think you can get it back from him?"

Coco shrugged.

"Maybe. But it's probably worth a shot."

"That would be something. Of course, I'd hate not seeing you, you know, not being able to have any more of our special sessions."

"Yeah. Tragic."

Agent Roberts laughed.

"So how was it?"

"How was what?"

"The story."

Coco brightened.

"It's a great story."

"Then what say you come back to bed for another round?"

"Baby, I'd love to, but I'm afraid you wore me out."

"Bullshit. Come on. Get your ass back in here. It's the perfect way to start the day."

Coco gave him a coy smile.

"Okay, but you need to shower first," she said, loosening the top button of her blouse.

"You got it, baby." He crushed out his cigarette, hopped out of bed and headed into the bathroom. Over the sound of running water, he said, "I won't be long."

"Take all the time you want."

Coco redid her top button, picked up her purse, and headed out the door.

19

A cool fall morning they'd enjoyed briefly during a stop for coffee, then back on the road. Casper's turn to drive, a job that long ago had *lost its allure*. Fucking guy always had to juice the conversation, couldn't possibly just say it straight, like how he didn't feel like driving, or this thing don't drive for shit in the wind, or how only a couple of hours behind the wheel just wore him the fuck out.

Either knew all about allure, but the only thing alluring about the Winnebago after four weeks on the road was Coco sleeping in the bedroom at sixty miles an hour. Either rode shotgun and offered helpful navigation tips-like 'Keep your eyes on the road or you'll get us killed' or 'Cop'-heading south to their next stop in San Jose; a place the Professor figured would have big stores with big rocks just waiting for them to drop by. A high probability for a lucrative haul, given all that tech money and the local residents' *propensity* to spend it.

Wanker.

Either watched the Professor check the speedometer, check his hair in the mirror then take a sip of coffee. As always, feeling in control and smug but preoccupied this morning. Probably with his lack of *writing output*, his *lagging word count*, comments that made Either feel like stabbing the guy in the neck with a fountain pen.

Who the hell talked like that?

"That was pretty amazing what she pulled off," Casper said.

Either laughed and nodded.

"Yeah. Poor old Chicken Wing never knew what hit him."

Casper nodded, then drifted off and stared out at the road in front.

"What's the matter with you?" Either said, shifting in his seat, trying not spill coffee on himself.

"Nothing," Casper said, glancing over a couple of times until he couldn't ignore Either's stare any longer. "Look, I'm fine. She did great."

"What is it with you two? Between your pouting like a baby and her being so pissed off at you...not that it hasn't been fun to watch, but enough is enough. It's getting on my nerves."

"It's nothing." He checked the outside mirrors, passed a semi, and eased the Winnebago back into the right hand lane. "It's just that I'm still not completely sure about her."

"What are you talking about?"

"Coco."

"What now? She hurt your *artistic sensibilities*? Make fun of your hairdo?"

"It's not a hairdo, it's a hair*style*. But that's not it. It's just a feeling I have that she's hiding something. It's like she's not being completely honest with us."

"Gee, a criminal who feels the need to hold shit back. Call 60 Minutes."

"Look, I get all that. But in this business you have to be able to trust your partners."

"So, I guess that means you're being completely honest with me?"

"Uh...sure."

"You hesitated."

"No, I didn't."

"What are you holding back?"

"Nothing."

Casper focused on the road. Either stared at him, then decided to let it go.

"We all got stuff to hide," Either said. "Man, I got shit I don't even talk with myself about." He finished his coffee. "But, so far, I haven't seen her do anything to make me not trust her. And believe me, I pay close attention to everything she does."

139

"That's because you're smitten."

"Why the fuck can't you ever just speak in plain English?"

"Let's just drop it, okay?"

"Maybe she's married. Or divorced and doesn't want us to know. Who gives a shit? Maybe she's walking around worried that something from her past is gonna reach out and grab her by her short and curlies."

"Yeah," Casper said, checking the outside mirror, not paying attention to the conversation. "If she had any."

"Yeah." Either nodded, then blinked and stared at Casper. "What?"

"What what?"

"You said, yeah, if she had any."

Casper, avoiding Either's stare, continued to focus hard on the outside mirror. "So?"

"So how would you know she doesn't have any?"

"Any what?"

"You're starting to piss me off, Professor. Any short and curlies."

"Oh. Just a guess."

"Bullshit."

"Look, Either."

"You prick. You slept with her."

"No, I didn't." Casper shrugged. "Not technically."

"What the hell does that mean?"

"Look," Casper said, glancing over his shoulder at the bedroom. "We promised not to talk about it."

"To who?"

"Who the fuck do you think? You. Who else wouldn't we not tell?"

"I can't believe it. You prick."

"Either, we didn't sleep together."

"Well, you must have done something."

"Yeah…well…ah, the hell with it. I'll tell you. Remember the other day when you went into town to do the food shopping? It was that afternoon. I should have been writing but…you know the drill…we started chatting, had a couple of cocktails, a little weed and, before we knew it we were in the bedroom."

"Goddamn it. I knew it."

"Funny, all the time we were in there, I don't remember seeing your name tattooed on her ass. So go fuck yourself."

"Then what happened?"

"We were getting real close to getting to it…right there, you know? She was stretched out in bed, her hair down, giving me that look and there I am, right there….you know?"

"Yeah, I got it. You and your throbbing manhood were right there."

"All the time I'm saying to myself that I couldn't believe it was actually finally going to happen, telling myself to relax. So I lie down next to her, stared into her eyes and said, 'I've wanted to do this since the first time I saw you…Gwen.'"

"Gwen? Who the fuck is Gwen?"

"Beats the hell out of me. Total brain cramp."

Either, laughing until tears formed in his eyes, said, "Man, you are so fucked."

"Tell me about it. I had my shot and completely muffed it."

"You muffed on the muff."

"My dream has turned into a haunting nightmare."

"Well, at least you got a bad metaphor out of the deal."

"I'll make it work."

"So she looked great, huh?"

"Unbelievable."

"No wonder she's been so pissed off."

"Yeah. I was hoping she'd eventually cool off, but I'm beginning to wonder. I've dug myself into a huge hole, and she's more than happy filling it up while I'm still down there."

They glanced back at the sound of the bedroom door opening. Coco, still sleepy, grabbed a bottle of orange juice, then sat down on the couch behind Either.

"How was your nap…Gwen?"

"Jesus, Either," Casper said, shaking his head, giving him a glare Either missed because he was beaming at Coco, a smile she missed while glaring at Casper.

"You just couldn't keep your mouth shut, could you?"

"He got it out of me."

"I've never been so embarrassed, never felt smaller in my entire life. And if you knew my mother, you'd realize just how fucking small that is."

"Really, Gwen. It's not that big of a deal."

"Either…don't start. Got it?"

The smile faded from his face and he nodded at her.

"Where's the vodka? This orange juice isn't cutting it," she said, heading to the kitchen. She poured a healthy shot into the juice bottle and sat back down, still glaring at Casper.

"Look, I admit it," Casper said. "I screwed up. But when you think about it, it's not really that big of a deal."

"Better let it go, Professor."

"No, I'm serious. What's the big deal? For example, take my name. Casper Dupree. See, it's just a name. No biggie. *Casper Dupree's Endless Book Tour*. It's got a nice ring to it."

"You're welcome," Either said.

Coco took a big slug of screwdriver.

"What's it mean?" she said.

"My name?" Casper said.

"Yeah."

"Casper Dupree?" Either said. "Means he probably got the shit kicked out of him in school."

Coco laughed. "We can only hope, right?"

Either laughed along.

Casper ignored them.

"Casper means *wealthy man*," he said. "And I loved the reference to Casper…you both remember Casper the Friendly Ghost, right? Given my career at the time, you know before I was an author, I thought that a wealthy man combined with a friendly apparition who comes and goes in the night really resonated…even had a hint of *gravitas*."

Coco snorted, pumped an air-fist up and down, then took another big slug of screwdriver.

"As soon as I put those two images together," Casper said, "I changed my name right away."

"You changed your name *to* Casper?" Coco said. "Really?"

Either smiled; no missing the '*you're fucking kidding me, right?*' meaning this time. Coco looked at him and nodded once.

"What about your name?"

"Mine? My name don't mean shit. It's just weird."

"Either Ore," she said, like she was trying it on for size. "I like it. But it must mean something."

"I did ask my old man about where it came from one time when I real young. He said it was because my mother could never make up her fucking mind about anything."

"Interesting," Coco said, draining the bottle. "Was that true?"

"Probably not, since she did eventually decide."

"About what?"

"Leaving."

Either stared out the window until she reached forward and touched his arm, bringing him back to the moment.

"You stay in touch with them?"

"Nah, both of them went their own way and pretty much disappeared into the vapor soon as they figured out that life wasn't like one of the Professor's books."

Coco nodded and removed her hand from his forearm.

"What did you do?" she whispered.

"Pretty much the same thing everybody else does. Just had to grow up real fast, and do it earlier than most other folks. Usual stuff; tried to survive, occasionally prosper a little."

"I'm so sorry, Either," she said.

"About what? Everybody's got a story."

"Yeah," she said, nodding.

"So what's yours?"

"My story? Not much to tell. My dad died a long time ago. My mother's around, but we're estranged."

"See? Everybody's got a story. Does Coco stand for anything?"

"Well, it's French and it means a pet name for something."

"Like, sweetie…sugar, something like that?"

"Yeah. After growing up under my mother's roof, I'm pretty sure that she eventually thought it meant the name of a pet. But given the way she drinks, I can understand the source of her confusion."

It was Either's turn to nod.

"They say that people with the name Coco have a deep desire to express themselves creatively. And I'm supposed to be affectionate and romantic and fall in love easily. But," she said, glaring at Casper, "people with my name also get their feelings easily hurt and have a quick temper."

"Yeah," Either said, "I've noticed that about you…Gwen."

Coco laughed.

"Oh, Either. What would I do without you?"

"Actually, Gwen, I'm a bit more interested in what you'll do with me."

Coco laughed harder and went to the kitchen to fix another screwdriver.

"To hear my mother tell it, she named me after Coco Chanel, the famous French fashion designer. But knowing her, she was probably just hammered at breakfast one morning, staring at a box of cereal."

She sat back down on the couch.

"She liked the sound of it. Thought it showed style, had resonance, maybe even a *hint of gravitas*. Coco Kinsley. Shit. What a joke."

Casper glanced over his shoulder.

"Did you say Kinsley?"

"Yeah."

"There's a Kinsley Publishing, one of the biggest publishers of romance novels on the planet."

"It's the biggest."

"Constance Kinsley, CEO of Kinsley Publishing, is your mother?"

"Yup. That's her. Good ole mom."

"Your mother owns one of the largest publishing houses in the world and we meet you working in a bookstore?"

"Maybe I believe in starting at the bottom and working my way up."

"You got plans to join the business?" Either said.

Coco rolled her eyes.

"Please tell me you're joking, Either."

"Well, if that's what you want to hear..."

"No, Either, I won't be joining the business. One time when I was about ten, one of my mom's friends asked me if I wanted to work with Mommy when I grew up. Before I could even open my mouth, my mother said that her plan was to get me started in small business. Then the ice queen said, 'Do you know how I'm going to set up Coco in a small business? I'm gonna give her a big one and wait.' Then she and her friend laughed and laughed and fucking laughed."

"I guess it's kinda funny," Either said.

"Not when you're ten."

"Why didn't you tell me she was your mother?" Casper said, tired of the trip down bad-memory lane, anxious to refocus the conversation.

Coco shrugged and gulped her screwdriver.

"I guess it didn't come up," she said.

"You didn't think it might be important to me?"

"Why would I? You're an independent. Why would an indie author care about a publisher the size of my mother's company?"

"You're joking, right? Forty percent of all the books sold on the planet are romance, and your mother sells about a quarter of them. Don't you think that I might be interested in getting a chance to meet with her? Show her my stuff?"

"Trust me. You don't want anything to do with my mother."

"Why on earth not?"

"Because you'd be making a deal with the devil, that's why."

"Don't you think that should be my decision?"

"Actually, it's my decision whether or not to ever introduce you to her. Let's not get ahead of ourselves here, Casper. Besides, we've got a good thing going here. Why would you do something stupid like getting involved with my mother and risk screwing everything up?"

"So you've got problems with your mother. Boo-fucking-hoo. Who doesn't? Shit, my mother only ever calls me for one of two reasons. One is to ask for money, the other is when she feels obligated to let me know someone in the family just died. And after she gives me the bad news about Uncle Fred, she asks for money."

"My situation is different," Coco said.

"I think you're exaggerating," Casper said.

"Look, the facts are that my mother hates books almost as much as she hates writers."

"She doesn't even know me. I'm sure I'd get along fine with her."

"Trust me, she'll hate you. But don't take it personally. She hates everybody. Except lawyers."

"Then what is she doing running a publishing company?" Casper said.

"She inherited it after my dad died."

"She could sell it."

"Sure, but that would deprive her of the two things she loves most. An endless stream of money and being surrounded by an army of sycophants she detests kissing her ass."

"Sycophant?" Either said.

"A self-serving, fawning parasite," Coco said, glancing at Casper.

"Oh," Either said, "Then I agree with the Professor. They'll probably get along just fine."

Coco laughed.

"I'm just asking you to think about introducing me. Could you do that?"

"Oh, I have been thinking about it, Casper."

"Really?"

"Yes, I have. And I'm thinking that it could be one of those moments in life that simply *resonates*."

Either laughed.

"Good one...Gwen."

20

*C*asper smiled and waved to several fans between careful sips of scalding coffee, tired, still preoccupied. But not bored; the man loved the attention, the sound of his own voice, and the sight of his signature inside the front cover. A seven o'clock signing tonight meant doing a solo; Either's term for a night when they didn't have any plans for a late night drop-in. Casper loved the solos since, tonight, everything was all about coiffed hair and tortoise-shell.

Either thought the solos were a waste of time since they distracted from their main mission, but the Professor had insisted saying they provided additional cover, enabled him to maintain the momentum the tour buzz was generating, give him a chance to focus on his fans and shine. Either wasn't sure about any of that, but the solos did give him the chance to generate a little buzz of his own. With nothing else to do but wait the evening out, he'd picked up a pint of bourbon he was now brown-bagging into his coffee.

Either glanced around the crowded bookstore between bites of sandwich, thinking back on how he'd gotten here, the several million in jewelry tucked behind the refrigerator; thinking about Amir down in L.A. and how he needed to call him; thinking about how long this thing might run, what he'd do next. Thinking about life in general; thinking about her. Looking for some answers to all the questions running through his head, questions now on fire from the bourbon-fueled coffee, but Either came up empty. As the Professor had eventually confirmed, like the panties, answers were scant.

"Now there's a metaphor."

"What?"

"Huh? Oh, nothing. Just thinking out loud."

"Don't hurt yourself," Casper said, giving him that 'aren't I clever' smile. Casper pointed at Either's chin. "You've got mayo on your face."

Either wiped with a napkin, looked at Casper for confirmation that he'd gotten it all, then glanced around the bookstore again.

"Good crowd," Either said. "I gotta hand it to you, Professor. This whole thing might have been my idea, but you're delivering the goods."

Casper studied the crowd of about a hundred.

"Yeah, it's okay. But just imagine how big it would be if I was signed with Kinsley."

"Shit. Just cool your jets. She said she'd talk with her."

"Well, she's certainly taking her time about it."

"Jesus, Professor, you spent the past week badgering her into it. She hasn't talked to her in almost seven years, and you expect her first conversation to be about some fucking writer."

"I am not just some fucking writer. Look at the size of this crowd."

Coco, talking on the phone, made her way to the table, nodding, speaking through clenched teeth. Either handed her his coffee. She smelled it, nodded thanks, and took a drink. Then took another.

"Yes. Uh-huh. Yes. Jesus Christ. Yes. I said yes, didn't I?"

She tossed the phone on the table and sat down.

"Was that her?" Casper said.

"Didn't you see the flames of hell shooting out of my phone?"

"That's great. What did she say?"

"I'm sorry, Casper, but I've got really bad news for you."

Crestfallen, Casper said, "Shit. You couldn't even get her to take a meeting?"

"Take a meeting?" Either said. "Sweet Jesus. Do you ever actually listen to yourself?" He looked at Coco. "You believe this guy? Who fucking talks like that?"

149

"I said I had bad news," Coco said, taking another drink of Either's coffee, then pointing at the cup. "I want one of those." She smiled at Casper. "She agreed to meet with you."

"Really? That's great. When?"

"At her annual conference next week in L.A."

"The Kinsley Connection Expo?"

"That's the one."

"Unbelievable. Thank you. Thank you so much, Coco."

Coco laughed.

"Don't say I didn't warn you."

"She agreed just like that?"

"Yeah, pretty much. Once we got through the initial mother daughter hate-fest."

"The dance of the scorpions?" Either said.

"Have you been working on your metaphors, Either?" Coco said, smiling at him.

"Hey, I pay attention," Either said, brown bagging another healthy shot of bourbon into his cup. He slid the cup in her direction.

"She's been following your tour. Said it was an amazing marketing ploy."

"You're welcome," Either said.

"That's great," Casper said.

"She also said it looks like you know how to sell books."

"Did she mention any specific books? Or talk about my writing style in general?"

"How many times do I have to tell you? She doesn't, and will never, give a shit about your writing style. The only question she needs answered is can you move product."

"This is great," Casper said. "Fan-fucking-tastic. Thank you."

Coco laughed again.

"There's more."

"More?"

"Yes, Professor. She's going to add you to an author panel. Wants to see how you handle yourself in front of a hostile crowd."

"Hostile crowd? What on earth is she talking about? My fans love me."

"She's not referring to your fans. She's talking about the other authors on the panel."

"You lost me."

"You're going to be on her annual Romance Symposium. It always ends up being the highlight of the conference."

"Wow. I'm honored. Must be an illustrious group of authors."

Coco laughed, louder this time, loud enough to make several people turn their heads toward the table.

"Not a chance. No author with half a brain would go anywhere near it."

"He'll fit right in," Either said.

"Exactly."

Casper glared at them.

"It's just one more example of my mother's perversity, that's all. Each year, she identifies four or five authors she's got under contract who hate each other's guts and puts them on a panel to duke it out over some stupid topic she's come up with."

"Sounds pretty boring to me," Either said.

"Oh, it would be without my mother's extra special touch to spice things up."

Casper and Either looked at her, waiting.

"Open bar."

"Really?" Either said. "Count me in."

"Open bar?" Casper said.

"Yeah. Three thousand people in the audience yelling and screaming at each other, most of them fans of the various authors; everyone, including the panelists, all liquored up and encouraged by my mother not to be shy about voicing their opinion."

"Better bring the Glock, Professor."

"It gets pretty wild." Coco chuckled. "I went to one seven years ago and swore I'd never do it again. But, for you, I just might have to make an exception."

Casper, now seeing his name in lights, pressed on.

"What's the topic of the panel?"

"Staying In or Straddling Lanes: Debating the Future of Sub Genre Purity in Romance."

Casper thought for a moment, then nodded.

"I think I'm pretty much a 'stay in your lane' kind of guy."

"Since you just keep writing the same book over and over," Coco said, "I'd have to agree."

"That is a gross generalization and is simply not the case."

"I wouldn't worry about it. Repetition's a skill that will come in handy. By the way, she's slotted you into the panel representing Romantic Suspense."

"I can make that work," Casper said, eyes dancing, fingers drumming the table. "This is exciting. Say, what's our schedule like before the conference?"

"We've got three, no four more signings and two…other jobs before then," Either said.

"I've got so much to do. Let's see…I'll need to get a haircut…and I should probably go clothes shopping…you guys think a suit would be too much, or should I just stick with the sports coat and jeans look?"

"You've created a monster," Either said, handing his coffee cup to Coco.

"The dumbass actually thinks I did him a favor."

They watched Casper, pondering and jotting notes down on a napkin. He chewed his pen, deep in thought, then leaned forward.

"Do we know anything about the jewelry stores that are coming up?"

"We know the same things we always do before we go in," Either said. "Why?"

"I hope they're high-end stores."

"Why do you care?" Coco said.

"Oh, I'd just like to pick up something nice for your mom."

21

*E*ither stepped onto the balcony and put his hands on the railing, marveling at the view of greater Los Angeles-as the hotel brochure called it-that stretched forever, wondering who decided it was greater. They'd driven past some pretty shitty neighborhoods on the way in this afternoon. And, he wondered, greater than what? He'd been in some pretty nice neighborhoods in his time. But yeah, he did have to admit that this part of greater L.A. was pretty great. Standing high above Rodeo Drive, with a mimosa in his hand Coco had made for them before she hit the shower, looking down at the people hustling with designer shopping bags. Everybody talking on their phones, paying no attention to the traffic as they crisscrossed the street, obviously thinking no one would fucking dare run them over as important as they were.

A lot of them spending more in an afternoon than he could steal in a week.

Either drained the mimosa. He walked back inside the suite and made another drink, this time a little heavier with the champagne. At eight hundred a bottle, he sure wasn't going to water it down with a bunch of OJ. He took a big gulp, topped the glass up, then put the bottle back in the fridge as he looked around the suite. Five thousand square feet, three bedrooms plus bathrooms that made the one in the Winnebago look like a port-a-potty.

Coco, wearing a robe and a towel wrapped around her head came out of the bathroom smiling and humming.

"Could I have another of these, please?"

She handed him her empty glass and Either refilled, taking time to top his off again.

"This place is amazing," Either said, handing her the fresh mimosa.

"Yes, it is. This is the hotel where they shot a lot of the scenes from *Pretty Woman*."

Either nodded, remembering Julia Roberts playing a hooker, but sure not looking like any hooker he'd ever come in contact with before. Richard Gere, sad, playing the hotel piano late at night, wondering how he's ever gonna be happy in life. Good looking, got all the money in the world, but the one thing he doesn't have is someone to share it all with. Boo-fucking-hoo. Then deciding all he needed to be happy was to settle down with a hooker. Like that happened all the time in real life. Of course, if the hooker was Julia Roberts, Either could understand the man's dilemma.

"How much does this suite go for?"

"I'm sure it's several thousand a night. But don't worry about it. My mother is paying for it."

"That was nice of her."

Coco snorted.

"Trust me, she didn't offer. It was part of our negotiation."

"As long as I'm not paying for it, I don't give a shit. It's incredible."

"It's a Four Seasons hotel."

"Yeah," Either said, glancing around. "I'd be pretty comfortable here no matter what time of year it was."

Coco stared at him, then laughed.

"Ah, Either. What am I going to do with you?"

"Well, from the looks of this place, we've got a lot of different rooms to find out."

Coco stopped laughing but maintained a small smile. She sat down on a couch, folded her legs under her, checked to make sure her robe was cinched, and patted the spot next to her.

"Sit down, Either. We need to talk."

"Hopefully a foreplay kind of chat."

She sipped her mimosa, then placed it on the coffee table in front of them. Either kept drinking his.

"If I thought for a minute you could handle that, Either, we would have done it weeks ago. In fact, we'd probably be doing it right now."

"What do you mean if I could handle it? You think I won't be able to flip your switch?"

"Flip my switch? Jesus, Either. Really?"

"You know what I mean."

"Yes, sadly, I do."

"So that's what you're talking about?"

"No, Either, it's not. I'm sure you'd be more than capable of flipping my switch." She shook her head and reached for her mimosa. "When I say you wouldn't be able to handle it, I'm talking about after."

"After? What's the problem? I usually just fall asleep."

"Jesus. No, after that. Like the next day. And beyond."

"What are you talking about?"

"Either, I'm afraid of you falling in love."

"A little late to start worrying about that now."

"Well, there you go," Coco said. "Then it would be a huge mistake for us to add sex to the mix." She put her glass back on the table and draped an arm across the top of the couch. "But I am so very fond of you, Either."

"Let me see if I've got this straight. You really like me, but somehow sleeping with me would change that?"

"Not for me. It wouldn't change a thing for me. It's you I'm worried about."

"You got some sort of policy against sleeping with guys you like?"

"Something like that, yeah."

"Then that explains your decision to get horizontal with the Professor."

"Yes, that one was all about my own pathologies. As much as Casper would like to think otherwise, he didn't do anything to charm the pants off me."

"And your scant lavenders?"

"Yes, them too." Coco removed the towel from her head and ran her fingers through her hair until it cascaded down her robe. "What you do think you're going to do after we wrap this thing up?"

"I was hoping we'd run off to someplace tropical and just kick back. Who knows, maybe knock out a couple kids at some point."

"You've got the wrong girl, Either," she said, her voice soft and serious, but still smiling. "I may be a smokin' hot piece of cooze but, trust me, I'm really fucked up."

"I'm posing as the business manager for a guy who writes romance novels and make my living knocking off jewelry stores. What's fucked up got to do with anything?"

"Good point."

"Besides, we can keep this thing going for a while. We got time to figure it all out."

"Either, Casper is wetting himself at the prospect of meeting my mother and getting a book contract out of her."

"So?"

"If he signs with her, our little adventure is over. She'll have him so far under her thumb he won't be able to breathe. And there's no way I would ever continue doing this if she were in the picture."

"You really think she's gonna offer him a contract?"

"It wouldn't surprise me at all. He's just her type. Eager and earnest and willing to sell his soul for a book deal."

"I need to meet this woman."

"Oh, you'll meet her. And it's funny now that I think about it. I think you're someone she'll tolerate. Maybe even find entertaining."

"But she won't like me."

"How many times do I have to tell you guys? She hates everybody."

"Maybe the Professor won't sign."

"We'll see. It'll be the standard contract she offers new writers."

"Well, it's a legal contract. It must give him some protection."

"Hah. I said it was her standard contract, I didn't say it was any good."

22

*C*oco grabbed Either's forearm just inside the entrance to the Exhibit Hall. He stopped and listened closely. She was talking different now, like she was back in a familiar yet foreign land she hadn't visited in a while. Talking about taking it all in before entering the throng, becoming just one more focused casual wanderer; whatever the fuck that meant. Her mother's term, not hers, she said, but not far from her own industry paradigm. Guiding him through the crowd and talking faster now, on a roll, probably nervous about seeing her mom after all these years, Either decided. Trying to overcome it by talking her way through it and by letting the environment influence her approach. Talking way too much about signings, appearances, workshops, vendor displays…way too much information for Either to process much less give a shit about. But, since it was her doing the talking, he was doing his best to pay attention as she kept chattering on, sounding like the Professor but without being smug about it.

A huge space – vast, the Professor would call it – filled with tables filled with books of all shapes and sizes, fans mingling with authors posing for pictures and getting their books signed.

Authors of all shapes and sizes, but the people on the covers similar. Pretty women looking vulnerable and pleading with their eyes to be rescued, swept away. Guys with muscles and no shirts staring out at the people walking by, some of them blown up to the size of posters and hanging on the wall. In front of them, signs labeling the person that wrote it, drew it, agented it, marketed it, or controlled East Coast distribution for it…all the information wearing him out, making his head throb.

"They pretty much all have the same expression on their face," Either said, staring up at the cover posters.

"That's because they're all saying the same thing."

"Buy the fucking book?"

"Exactly."

Coco squeezed his arm and pointed as Casper approached, in jeans and a black T-shirt underneath a new dark blue sports coat. He looked past them, beaming and waving to a couple of people who might have been waving at him. The Professor, not taking any chances, waved again. He stopped and smiled, a goofy look on his face. He adjusted the bridge of his tortoise-shell glasses.

"This is unbelievable," he said. "I can't thank you enough, Coco."

"The pleasure is all mine," she said, giving him a strange smile he was having trouble deciphering.

"Almost time," he said, glancing down at his watch, tapping a foot, scanning the room and making sure the smile never left his face. "Think she'll be on time?"

"My mother's never late," Coco said. "But when you believe you actually control the passage of time, being late becomes impossible."

The Professor nodded, but Either, head throbbing, didn't have the energy to try and figure out what philosophical or *metaphysical* point she was making.

"When's the bar open?"

"One o'clock sharp," she said. "Don't worry, as soon as we get Casper and my mother rolling, that's where we're headed."

"Good," Either said, glancing around the room, thinking a cold beer would go down good.

Either watched Coco's face drop, her body seeming to collapse into itself for a second. She took several deeps breaths, straightened her back and stood tall. An elegant woman approached, trailed by several young men and women all trying to stay right behind her, but not close enough to do something stupid like step on her foot. Or her shoes, which Either guessed, cost more than his car.

Mid to late-fifties, he decided, still looking good. An older version of Coco. Either just stood quietly and waited his turn.

Coco leaned in and whispered in Either's ear.

"Just don't get to close."

"Doesn't like her personal space invaded?"

"No, she's a biter," she whispered, then laughed. "Relax, you'll be fine." She took one more deep breath, then turned and smiled. A fake smile, Either decided, but not bad.

"Hello, Mother."

"Coco, darling, it's been far too long."

Either watched them hug; he'd come in closer contact with dogs, and he was scared to death of them.

"Your father would be amazed at how you've turned out...I know I certainly am."

"Yes, I remember him telling me how proud he was on his death bed."

"Well, he was pretty sick at the end, perhaps hallucinating."

She laughed at her own joke, the crowd standing behind her nervously glancing back and forth, wondering whether to join in or not. Choosing silence rather than risk getting it wrong, they shuffled their feet and glanced around the room.

Coco glared at her mother who stood there giving it right back, the immediate area seeming quieter now to Either.

Dance of the scorpions indeed.

He glanced at the Professor who was starting to sweat right through his sports coat, then checked his watch, wanting the bar to be open.

"Have you had some work done, darling?"

"No, mother, this is the real me." Coco beamed. "But I can understand your confusion...knowing how many years it's been since you've seen the real thing."

"I see...so it's going to be one of *those* conversations is it?"

"That's completely your call, Mother."

161

"Oh, I'm so glad to hear that. Let's save that one for later, shall we?" She glanced at Casper and Either, seeing them for the first time. "I believe we have a spot of business to take care of, right?"

"Indeed." Coco turned and extended an arm in the Professor's direction. "Mother, I'd like you to meet Casper Dupree. Of the endless book tour fame."

"Yes, of course," she said, shaking Casper's hand, staring into his eyes like she was trying to burn a hole in his head. "My God," she said, shaking her head. "You might as well call it the endless root canal. And on a bus?" She turned her head and glanced back at her entourage. "Just fucking kill me now, right?"

The entourage coughed up a nervous chuckle, then fell silent.

"It is so nice to meet you, Mrs. Kinsley," Casper said. "No, allow me to rephrase that. It's an honor to meet you."

"Hmmm," she said, letting go of Casper's hand. "Coco always was a very good judge of character."

"Well, thank you," Casper said, beaming, pressing a finger against the bridge of his glasses.

"Not at all. You earned it," she said. "Sycophantic combined with self-absorption is a tough one to pull off."

"It's a Winnebago."

Everyone turned to stare at Either.

"I beg your pardon?" she said, sizing him up.

"It's a Winnebago, not a bus."

"I see. And you must be…what? The chauffeur?"

"I said it's a Winnebago, not a limo. I'm his business manager."

"Really?"

No mistaking the 'You're fucking joking, right?' meaning this time – just put it right out there, hit him right in the nuts with it.

"It's nice to see that her good looks aren't the only thing Coco gets from you," Either said.

Coco laughed and grabbed Either's arm. "Good one. Mother, I'd like you to meet Either Ore."

"Either or what?"

"Either or fucking nothing. It's spelled O. R. E."

"Well, butter my butt and call me a biscuit. Dumb *and* feisty. I do like that in a man." She turned to Coco. "He's delicious, darling." She glanced back over her shoulder at her entourage. "Remind me later to follow up with our Mr. Either Ore."

A woman dressed in corporate dark blue glanced down at an appointment book she was holding. "What time?"

"Really, Josie?" She shook her head, glaring at the woman, who was trying to disappear into the appointment book. "Really? Now I have to actually *define* what *later* is?"

She shook her head at her entire entourage, dismissing them with a wave of her hand.

"All of you go away. You're such a fucking disappointment. Go away and do something useful, like selling some books. That's why we're here, right? Or will I need to remind all of you about that *later*?"

They scurried off, whispering among themselves, blaming Josie for pissing her off.

"Okay, Casper Dupree of the endless book tour fame on a…Winnebago, we need to chat." She turned to Coco. "I'm sure we'll be seeing each other later on, darling. Perhaps at the panel?"

"Mother, I wouldn't miss that for the world."

"Good. I have a feeling it's going to be extra special this year. Try to come early and get a good seat. That is, if you can tear yourself away from the bar."

"I'll do my best, Mother, but I do love drinking all your booze."

"Yes, I remember it well. And you, Mr. Either Ore spelled O-R-E, I will be seeing you later as well. I can't wait to hear all about where you came up with the endless book tour concept. It's quite brilliant."

"Yes," Casper said, "It certainly helped me gain some very valuable exposure. I have to admit having some regrets about it coming to an end."

"Coming to an end? Oh, no-no-no. Why on earth would we do something so positively stupid as that? No-no-no, we need to build on it. Maintain the momentum."

"Uh, what do you mean?" Casper said, confidence fading fast, sweat stains emerging under the arms of his jacket.

"Let's save that for *later*. It will give us something to talk about after we get through some of the initial contract terms."

"Contract?" Casper said, recovering.

"Why, of course. Did you think I agreed to meet with you just to *chat*?" she said, glancing at Either. "I'm assuming you don't have any problem with me talking contracts with Mr. Dupree."

"He's all yours," Either said. "Knock yourself out." Then, remembering something Coco had said on their way over to the conference, "We can talk about my buyout clause later on."

She didn't make a sound, but Either knew he'd connected; a quick jab that went straight from her ear to her gut. Seconds later, she recovered and managed a smile. "Wonderful," she said. "Come Mr. Dupree. Let's go see if we can predict your future. See you later at the panel, darling."

In total control, she led Casper away by the arm. It reminded Either of a cop escorting a perp into the back seat of a car.

"Careful you don't bump your head, Professor."

Coco and Either watched them disappear through a door near the entrance to the Exhibit Hall.

"He's fucked," Either said.

"Exactly."

"It's one o'clock."

"Actually, it's two minutes past."

Coco led Either by the arm in the direction of the bar.

23

*C*asper stood behind a curtain with three other panelists, two of them already threatening to punch each other, calling each other dickhead and bitch between gulps of margarita. Casper was on his third, still trying to clear his head and focus after his whirlwind thirty minute conversation. Actually he hadn't done much of the talking with his new boss; new owner was more like it, he conceded.

He checked the inside pocket of his jacket, brushed his fingers against a copy of his new contract. Casper smiled, trying to maintain that feeling of being special, hanging onto that initial flush of excitement. He worried the initial smidgen of dread that'd taken root at the exact moment he'd signed his name on the thirty-page document written in a miniscule-font foreign language was about to spread into a full-blown virus.

Not a bad metaphor, he decided; maybe he could use that.

Or perhaps save it for his autobiography. A writing project he should probably start soon if he was going to work for her.

She'd been charming; he was the defanged snake slowly rising out of a basket.

She'd been all-business. A total pro. He was the rookie, just called up to the majors, trying to hang with her, but quickly realizing he'd be lucky to hit two hundred against her even if she just brought heat and didn't throw any curves.

She'd been forceful; he looked at the sales report she casually slid across the table and crumbled. Completely folded and collapsed from the sheer size of the numbers and her promise of marketing support and international exposure.

She'd been flattering, occasionally bordering on obsequious, showing off a bit, doing a demonstration for him in case he needed to use the skill in the future. As if saying, 'That's how you play the sycophant, Mr. Dupree.'

He'd been dumb enough to fall for it, walked right into it by asking her which books of his she'd read, which one was her favorite.

That was when the smidgen of dread had first appeared. She'd said, "What difference does it make? In the end, they're all the same fucking book." Hit him right between the eyes with that one, keeping him off balance. Yet still anxious to get his hands on the contract sitting right in front of her on the table. She teased him with it, making him wait.

She'd slid the contract across the table while talking about two hundred grand as an advance and fifteen percent royalties until he'd *earned out*. How it could bump it to seventeen, maybe even twenty, but not to worry about that level of detail now, they would have plenty of time to talk about that *later*. After he'd seen how increased sales quickly overcame any *perceived* loss of income based on his current royalty percentage he had as an indie.

"Besides," she'd said, crocodile-smiling over the rim of her water glass, "We'll have three-years to figure all that out."

Talking faster, but not missing a beat, not missing a word. Even her breathing was timed to not break the flow; flipping a page, providing a quick summary, then on to the next. Lathered, rinsed, repeated her way through all thirty pages, then sat back in her chair smiling. She slid a gold pen across the table that shone in the fluorescent light and beckoned. Casper looked down at the pen and his name printed on the signature page, then looked back at her.

"Maybe I better have my lawyer take a look at it first," he'd said, faking his way through the fact that he didn't have one. He figured that finding representation right outside the door would be about as hard as finding something to read.

"Really?"

166

She'd stared at him across the table, maintained a smile as her eyes turned black. Casper felt a sudden chill in the air he hoped was the air conditioning.

"Certainly," she'd said, "I understand completely. It's just such a pity you won't be able to participate on the panel." Now beaming as she saw him fidget upon hearing that little nugget, she said, "Oh, didn't Coco mention that to you?" She continued on about how she had a strict company policy she wished there was something she could do about, how only *signed* authors could participate on that particular panel, due to the massive exposure it provided annually to those authors taking part.

She had him right where she wanted him: by the balls, with a healthy portion of his short-and-curlies thrown in for good measure.

She'd felt it coming the moment he'd hesitated on the lawyer.

But when she saw the look on his face about missing the panel, she knew she had him.

And he knew it too.

Casper had listened to the crowd getting louder, fueled by alcohol and anticipation, sounding more like a crowd at a rock concert than a book convention. He nodded at her, exhaled loudly, felt the immense weight of the pen in his hand, and signed the contract.

Standing behind the curtain now, three margaritas down, his thinking was still jumbled but feeling a bit better.

Maybe that was the solution, he thought; just keep drinking.

It's only three years.

Shit, Either had done three years in a much tougher place.

That *had* to be tougher than being under contract with her, right?

And he'd come through it okay.

Still dumb as a box of rocks, but that wasn't entirely his fault.

Casper started thinking back on the Tour, about how much fun they'd had, how much shit they'd stolen, how much money they'd have once it was all fenced. But after looking at the numbers she'd provided earlier, even at fifteen percent, he'd be making enough. Probably nowhere near as much as he could make knocking off jewelry stores but, without the threat of being sent away for twenty years.

He was sure he could adjust.

And it was only three years.

He could do that standing on his head.

Right?

Casper turned as she touched his arm.

"I hope you have a nice buzz going, but not too big. I want you relaxed, but stay sharp out there."

"Got it. I'm fine."

"Good. If everything goes to plan, by tonight you'll be a household name."

"What?"

But she cut him off with a wave of her hand.

"Shhh. It's showtime."

And then she burst through the curtain to thunderous applause.

**

"Los Angeles? Are you ready?"

Another thunderous burst of applause.

"Romance lovers? Are you ready?"

Another sustained burst.

"That's great! Hey, I need to ask you something. How's the open bar treating you?"

A standing ovation that ran for two minutes.

**

Either and Coco, sitting in the cordoned-off section reserved for her mother's staff, ducked and weaved away from cups of ice, pamphlets and the occasional paperback that flew past their heads.

"Jesus," Either said. "They're going nuts."

"You haven't seen anything yet. Wait until they get their eyes on the Professor."

Either looked at her and waited for more.

"Fresh meat," she said.

"You think he signed the contract?"

"He won't be up there if he didn't."

"He wouldn't miss this. He'll be up there."

"Exactly."

"She knows how to work a crowd."

"She fucking knows how to work everything." Coco drained her martini, felt the buzz emerge, then rubbed her forehead and blinked. "Except kitchen appliances. Somehow, those she never managed to master."

"How many of those have you had?"

"Not nearly as many as I'm going to. Why don't you ask the waiter to bring us two more see-throughs?"

"I don't want to miss anything."

"Don't worry, the preliminaries will run awhile."

**

"I'm so glad you're having a great time."

Waiting for the applause to build, then subside.

"Yes, we've got so many great books here at Kinsley, so many great authors…and it is such an honor and a privilege for me to able to bring them to you in this great setting. How about a nice round of applause for the staff of the Los Angeles Convention Center for all their hard work?"

Leading the applause, then waiting again for the room to get quiet.

"Yes, we've all been working so hard to get ready for this. I know that I personally have spent so much time pulling together the displays for literally thousands of books that you've spent the past two days exploring, browsing, reading…buying."

A coy smile held through the applause and laughter.

"Yes, we've been working so hard making sure all the books and authors were ready to go…that we had enough booze and appetizers to keep you happy. Yes, yes, you're very welcome."

Turning serious now.

"But I'm sorry to say, I have to give you a bit of bad news, folks."

A collective Scooby Doo '*Ruh-Roh*' from the audience followed by laughter. A familiar moment for the veteran conference goers, knowing from experience that something good was coming.

"Yes, that's right, folks. Bad news. I hope you all know that I'm more than happy to provide all the Scooby Snacks…and books hot enough to make your skin melt…and enough booze to get a crowd of three thousand nice and toasty. Yes, I can get each and every one of you in the mood… but you are going to have to do some of the heavy lifting here. I can't do everything, right? Simply put…I can't get you laid."

A burst of laughter and applause that built, sustained, then grew louder.

"We love you, Constance."

She scanned the audience in a mock-search for the speaker, then said, "Constance? Really? That's Mrs. Kinsley to you. Surely you guys know that by now."

On cue, the audience roared then said in unison:

"Yes, we know. And don't call me Shirley."

Another burst of laughter and applause, punctuated with a flurry of flying plastic cups.

**

"Has she been drinking?" Either said as the waiter handed them fresh martinis.

"God, no. Having three thousand people in the palm of her hand is all the buzz she needs."

Either nodded.

"She'll drink later," Coco said, downing half of her fresh see-through.

**

"Okay, enough of this. Let's get to work."

Pacing the stage, getting her thoughts together.

"You know…over the years I've seen so many changes in the world of the romance novel. And while the genre, and certainly Kinsley Publishing, stays faithful to its origins, the lines have blurred. So as I was starting to think about this year's Free for All – and for all you first timers, I'm talking about the name of the panel, not the price of the books."

Waiting out the laughter, feeling the energy she fully controlled, knowing she could ask all of them to roll over and play dead, she stood in the center of the stage waiting.

"As I was putting the panel together, I thought, how about bringing together four authors who represent various romance sub-genres and asking them what they thought about where the future would lead our industry? And the types of books you'd be seeing over the coming years. And then I hit on the topic of: *Staying In or Straddling Lanes; Debating the Future of the Romance Sub-Genre.*"

Pausing for a quick burst of applause.

"So it is my pleasure to introduce this year's Free for All panel. First up, I'd like to introduce someone you all know and love, one of Kinsley's longtime Christian Romance authors, a real *stay in her own lane* kind of girl…because that's what Jesus would do. Please join me in welcoming a writer who assures me that the sales performance of her last book was a one-time aberration and that there won't be any Second Coming of that momentous event, ladies and gentlemen, Christine Florentine."

**

"Wow," Either said. "She's brutal. Thanks for coming, but don't let the door hit you in the ass on the way out."

"Yeah," Coco said, holding up two fingers to the waiter. "Her contract is about to expire, and Mommy Dearest wants her to cut her royalty percentage before agreeing to a new one."

"Her sales are dropping?"

"Her last book sold twelve copies less than the previous one. And like mother always tells her authors…If your sales aren't going up, you're going down."

"Man, tough gig. She looks nervous up there."

"Gee, I can't imagine why. A born-again Christian writer surrounded by three thousand screaming drunks."

"Good point."

**

"Next, I'd like to bring out someone who needs no introduction."

Pausing, looking at her watch, staring at the curtain, then shaking her head at the audience.

"That's your cue, Larry."

Waiting until a bald guy, looking more like a truck driver than a romance novelist, poked his head through the curtain, still uncertain about whether to come out on stage or not.

"Ladies and gentlemen, Larry Withers."

Tentative applause, the audience wanting to applaud, but not for just the guy's bald head.

"C'mon out, Larry. I'm just having a little fun with you."

If Larry was having any fun, it wasn't apparent to the audience. Carrying a margarita, he gave her a dark glare and sat down next to the Christian writer, now grasping her water glass with both hands shaking, probably hoping it would turn into wine.

"Larry isn't known for his sense of humor, folks. Right, Larry?" Turning to the audience, saying, "See those daggers he's giving me? If he had used daggers half as well in his last book he might have really had something there. What was the title, Larry? *Chutes and Daggers*? Yeah, that was it. Historical adventure romance based on a popular children's game if I remember the blurb. A real page turner. And, fortunately for all his readers, short."

Turning to the audience.

"Sixty thousand words. Is that too much to ask?"

"No," the audience roared.

Turning back to Larry, pounding his margarita, his mood turning darker by the minute.

"It's not like I ask you to count them yourself. There is technology available that will do that for you, Larry. What was the final word count? Fifty thousand?"

"Fifty-two," Larry whispered.

"Yeah, that's right, fifty-two. And how long is the new one going to be, Larry?"

"Sixty-eight."

"Good boy, Larry."

A rumble in the audience from a group of Larry's fans sitting near the stage.

"Leave him alone. You're being rude."

She looked out into the audience and smiled.

"Well, it's about time, people. Have you forgotten this particular panel is called the Free for All? I thought I was going to have mention Larry's latest stint in rehab to get your attention."

Looking at Larry, then back at the audience, now beaming.

"Oops," she said, and placed a hand over her mouth.

"Bitch," Larry whispered.

She heard it, but let it pass without comment.

"Larry's background is in Historical Romance, but he's been one of our biggest experimenters working with multiple sub-genres. I thought he'd be perfect for today's session representing the straddling-lanes perspective. Let's welcome Larry with another round of applause."

A short burst of polite applause interspersed with hoots and hollers from Larry's fan base.

**

"Man, she *is* brutal," Either said. "His contract up for renewal?"

"No, she just hates his guts."

"Why does she keep him around?"

"Because he moves product, Either. Jesus, pay attention when I tell you things."

"Don't yell at me."

"Sorry." She patted his arm and rested her head on his shoulder briefly.

"You're in a mood."

"Yeah. I call it the Mommy Dearest see-through effect."

"Well, don't fucking take it out on me."

"Shhh. I'm sorry. Okay?"

Either drained his glass and held up two fingers to the waiter.

**

"Next, I'd like to bring out someone I absolutely adore."

**

"As long as she keeps selling truckloads of books," Coco said.

174

"This woman, unlike Larry, who you might not recognize even if you lived with him, truly needs no introduction."

**

"Jesus, Mother. Leave the guy alone."
"It's almost like she's trying to provoke him."
"Wow. Of course. That's exactly what she's doing. Either, that's brilliant."
"That's better."
She kissed him on the cheek and accepted a fresh see-through from the waiter.

**

"Almost single-handedly, she has built and sustained Kinsley's Paranormal Romance market share. Her vampires are hot, real, and well…what can I tell you? You have to read it to believe it…but trust me, they're smoking hot. Ladies and gentlemen, please welcome… Vanessa."
A raucous standing ovation for a vivacious woman in her thirties stuffed into leather, a tattoo of two puncture marks and blood dripping down the side of her neck. She beamed and waved, then sat down in the chair furthest from Larry.

**

"Just the one name?"
"Yeah. She dropped her last name several years ago as a marketing strategy."
"It must have worked. It's totally her crowd, huh?"
Coco nodded.
"Yeah, she moves a ton of product. I can't read her stuff, but I like her because she's the only author with Kinsley who can get away with telling my mother to go fuck herself. The

only appearances she makes are the ones spelled out in her contract. Doesn't do interviews. Let's her writing speak for her as she likes to say. Very private, refuses to divulge anything about herself, especially her sexuality."

"Keeps all the men and the women guessing, huh?"

"Exactly."

"Smart."

"Very smart. And one more reason for my mother to hate her."

Coco leaned forward in her chair.

"Okay, here we go."

**

"And finally, it is my distinct pleasure to introduce to you our final panelist, a special surprise for all of you, the newest member of the Kinsley family. Someone I just signed to an exclusive three-year contract this afternoon."

Pausing to let the buzz in the room build.

"A gentleman, and yes, ladies, that is exactly what he is…a gentleman of the finest quality. Not to mention the fact that he is absolutely gorgeous, someone you may have seen recently, or had the distinct pleasure of meeting, traveling the country on his Endless Book Tour…"

The buzz swelling, turning into applause of anticipation – 'Could it be?' – 'I can't believe it's him, no way.'

**

"Son of a bitch," Either said, staring around the room, engulfed by the groundswell of applause.

"This is all because of you. You know that, right? You made it happen for him, Either."

"I did, didn't I?"

She patted his arm, took a slug of her martini, and smiled to herself.

**

"Okay, let's get him out here, people. Ladies and gentlemen, please join me in welcoming to the stage, Casper Dupree!"

Casper stepped through the curtain, at first tentative, then getting into it. Overwhelmed by the applause, but digging it, letting it wash over him. The kind of applause he always imagined he'd get if he could ever tell a crowd of people about how he and Either had done their thing. He sat down between Vanessa and Larry and waved at the crowd until the applause faded.

"Let's get started, shall we? Okay, first question. And let's start by getting the Christian Romance perspective. Christine, as an author what is your approach to the question of staying in your lane or letting yourself go and incorporating elements of other romance sub-genres into your work?"

"Well," Christine said, "I believe…"

"Yes, dear, we all know that."

Nervous laughter from the audience.

**

"Jesus Christ, she's not going to go after the Christian is she?"

"No, never in public. She's just warming up."

**

"Yes, of course," Christine said, forcing a nervous chuckle. "As a believer, I find that the Bible provides such breadth and depth, is such a complete canvas of human emotions like love, honor and respect. I simply don't feel the need to look elsewhere for elements found in all Romance novels."

"You don't find it limiting?" Larry said, reaching for the pitcher of margaritas on the table.

"No, not at all," Christine said. "My books are all about romance and love. It's just that in mine, in addition to loving each other, my characters just happen to share a love of Jesus."

A quick burst of polite, respectful applause from the audience, along with a couple of 'Thank ya, Jesus' tossed in from Christine's small, but ardent, fan base.

Larry snorted loudly and tossed back half a margarita.

"There's no need to be disrespectful, Larry," Christine said.

"Christian romance," he said, starting to slur, "is total schlock."

"Well," Vanessa said, seizing the opening. "If there's anybody up here who would recognize schlock, it would be you, Larry."

The crowd roared. It subsided and left most of the audience leaning forward in their chairs.

"Hey, Gruzilla, or whatever you're calling yourself this week, why don't you just sit back and wait your turn?"

"Wait for my turn? Now there's a typical chauvinistic response. Of course, what would we expect from someone who sets his books in centuries old-settings where the dominance of the male wasn't even discussed, much less challenged? "

Vanessa refilled her margarita and raised her glass to the audience. She glanced at Larry and said, "Fucking redneck."

"What is it with you? You're just jealous because you aren't capable of writing in multiple sub-genres."

"Hah." She looked out at the audience. "This coming from a guy who couldn't write his way from point A to B with GPS and a guide dog."

The audience roared, and a burst of crushed paper cups filled the air.

"Let me give you a piece of career advice, Larry. You might try learning how to write in one genre before trying to handle multiples. No, allow me to rephrase. You might actually try learning how to write."

"Bite my ass."

"Sorry, Larry, but I'll wait for lunch. Besides, you're not my Type."

Vanessa turned to the audience and waited for the joke to sink in. The laughter built and was followed by a nice round of applause.

"Thanks," Vanessa said. "I'll be here all week. And don't forget to tip your waiters and bartenders. Which reminds me," she said, holding up the empty margarita pitcher. "We're gonna need at least one more of these."

She sat back in her chair, smiling.

"I simply don't understand why you continue to trash my books. For someone who says she likes to keep a low profile, we certainly do hear a lot from you when it comes to my work."

"What can I tell you, Larry? Trashing your work is one of life's greatest pleasures."

Another burst of laughter, punctuated with shouts of protests from Larry's fans that were quickly drowned out.

"It's the fact that I cut into your territory, isn't it?"

"Please," Vanessa said. "Your books are dog-crap-scented doorstops."

"You're one to talk," Larry said, grabbing the fresh pitcher from the waiter and refilling his glass. "All you do is write the same vampire story over and over and over."

"Hey, it's called writing accuracy based on solid research. At least my vampires know how to stay in character."

"Hah," Larry said, slurping down a healthy slug of margarita. "You just hate it when other authors have the audacity to incorporate Paranormal into their work."

Larry turned to the audience.

"My new one is an historical-Christian-paranormal romance opus called, *Bite, Pray, Love*. It's quite edgy."

"Edgy?" Vanessa said, lighting a cigarette. "It's a piece of shit."

"I don't think you can smoke in here," Christine said.

"Hey, Church Lady, mind your own business. It's in my contract."

"Really?" she said, glancing at Mrs. Kinsley, now sitting in a chair off to one side of the stage, enjoying the show. She nodded at Christine and lit a cigarette of her own.

"You don't know what you're talking about," Larry said, glaring at Vanessa. "I'm telling you, *Bite, Pray, Love* is an amazing example of how multiple Romance sub-genres can be woven together into a coherent narrative."

"Your main character is a vampire who bites Jesus in the neck and finds God."

"What's wrong with that?"

"You set the fucking thing in 300 BC." Vanessa turned to the audience. "Oops. Sorry, folks. Spoiler alert."

The crowd roared with laughter.

"300 BC?" Christine said. "Oh, my Lord. I'm sorry but that would simply require readers to make too much of a leap of faith."

"Hey, Church Lady," Vanessa said, "did I ask for your help?"

"I was merely commenting on the gross historical inaccuracy," Christine said.

"It also has elements of fantasy I neglected to mention," Larry said to Vanessa before turning on Christine. "And you. Just stay out of this. Talk about staying in your lane. Christine, have you ever even *heard* of the concept of conflict? All your characters do is sit around and tell each other how much they love each other, how they love Jesus, and how much Jesus loves them."

"My readers certainly seem to enjoy my work."

"Good for them. I gotta tell you, Christine, Jesus may love *you*, but I'm pretty sure he hates your books."

"There's no need to be cruel. I write Christian Romance. What do you expect my characters to do? Have a chariot race? Really, Larry, in your last book you had chariots racing at eighty miles an hour."

"How many times do I have to explain it to you people? At the risk of repeating myself, it's a *fantasy*-historical-adventure."

"At the risk of repeating myself," Vanessa said, "it's a piece of shit."

"It's about creating alternative realities. You know, what might have been."

"Well, sure," Vanessa said, topping up her glass. "That explains everything. And I guess if Jesus can get bitten in the neck by a vampire three hundred years before he even shows up, anything's possible."

"It's called suspension of disbelief. Maybe you should try it sometime."

"Oh, believe me, Larry, I've tried," Vanessa said. "But every time I do, I always remember that you're a published author and the whole construct falls apart."

It took several minutes for the audience to stop laughing. When the room quieted down, Vanessa turned to Larry.

"Your turn."

"You're a hack who overwrites everything," Larry said.

"Now you're just reaching," Vanessa said. "A little desperate, Larry."

"Actually," Christine said. "You do have a tendency to overwrite."

Vanessa leaned forward and looked down the table.

"Could someone please pass the margarita pitcher?" Casper said, dying to find a way into the debate.

"Get it yourself," Vanessa said.

"Yeah, Romance Boy," Larry said. "And make yourself useful and refill mine while you're at it."

"Maybe you two should dial it down a notch," Casper said, glancing back and forth between Larry and Vanessa sitting on opposite sides of him.

"Shut up, *Casper*," Vanessa said. "The guy's been under contract for about an hour and already thinks he's gonna dictate. He must be dizzy from smelling all those bus fumes."

"It's not a bus. It's a Winnebago."

"The temerity," Larry said. "Mr. Throbbing Manhood thinks he's gonna call all the shots."

"It's a metaphor."

"No shit, Sherlock," Larry said.

Vanessa continued to stare down the table at Christine.

"So you think I overwrite, do you?"

"Yes. Perhaps a little."

"Wow," Larry said. "That's quite a criticism coming from you."

"What do you mean?" Christine said.

"You spent nine pages describing a set of rosary beads in your last book," Larry said. "You made Tom Clancy sound like Hemingway."

"Could someone please pass the pitcher of margaritas?"

"Shut up," Vanessa said, glaring at Casper, then turning to Larry. "You're one to talk about overwriting. Why don't you try *showing* once in a while instead of just telling your readers what they're seeing?"

"I'm the writer. Who else would tell them?"

"What a fucking moron."

"That's it," Larry said, jumping to his feet, arm cocked, ready to launch a punch over Casper into Vanessa's snarling face. Casper stood, intercepted Larry's arm, twisted it behind his back, and grabbed him by the belt in one move. He dragged Larry over the table to the front of the stage and tossed him into the front row.

A stunned silence followed by a small round of applause built into a sustained standing ovation. Casper, stunned by the audience's reaction, worked his way back to his seat and peered over the front of the stage anxiously waiting for Larry to emerge. First day under contract, he decided, was probably not the best time to kill another author, especially one that moved product.

**

"That was pretty slick," Either said.

182

"Yeah," Coco said, nodding. "That Sir Galahad routine will, as my mother says, *resonate*." She laughed and shook her head. "Gotta hand it to her. She set the whole thing up, and it played out perfectly."

Either glanced at Coco, her eyelids drooping. She gave him a goofy grin.

"Another see-through, my good man."

"I don't think that's a good idea."

"Why not? We're not driving."

"One more of those and you won't even be walking."

"Maybe comatose is the effect I'm going for."

**

"Ladies, did I not tell you what a gentleman he was?"

Another round of applause.

Casper caught the slight nod his new boss gave him. He stood, walked to the center of the stage.

"Thanks, everyone. But I think there are just certain boundaries you don't cross."

The applause continued.

Casper, seizing the moment, adjusted his tortoise-shell glasses and looked out at the audience.

"I think maybe we should forget for a moment all the various sub-genres, all this stuff about lane shifting, and remember why we all love Romance novels in the first place. For example, take my books…they're stories about redemption, about people striving to overcome long odds, stories about love. But mostly, all my books are about people trying to find happiness amid a sea of life's challenges. Redemptive, uplifting, timeless, enduring love…those are the things I write about. And I write about those things because I know that's what you all love to read."

Another sustained standing ovation ensued. As it continued, Casper's new boss approached and draped an arm over his shoulder.

"Ladies and gentlemen, I am so proud to present to you the new Bad Boy of Romance, Casper Dupree. A man who not only writes about the defense and protection of women, but, as you've all just witnessed firsthand, also lives out that value in his daily life. I strongly encourage all of you to stay tuned for the first installment in his new series, coming soon from Kinsley Publishing, *Ram Johnson: In and Out of Trouble*."

One more standing ovation that left Casper beaming at the audience, adjusting his glasses, touching his hair.

"And on that note, I'd like to thank you for coming today. Lunch is ready, so enjoy yourself."

Nobody in the audience moved. Casper continued to preen, amazed that the audience was refusing to leave, and wondered if he should offer up another burst of sage advice. Mrs. Kinsley studied Casper's reaction and smiled.

"Oh, what the hell," she said to the audience, laughing. "Let's say keep the bar open for another couple of hours, too."

The audience roared and jumped out of their seats, streaming towards the exits.

She turned her microphone off, then looked at Casper, now flushed with embarrassment.

"Well done, Mr. Dupree," she said. "But never forget one thing. You might be one of the stars, but I own the sky."

"Got it," Casper whispered, staring down at the stage, then looking at her. "Can I ask you a question?"

"Of course."

"Who the hell is Ram Johnson?"

"Why, he's the superhero of your new series."

"New series?"

"This would probably be a good time for you to read your contract."

"Ram Johnson?"

"It's a metaphor," she said, laughing. "It has a nice ring to it, don't you think?"

"In and out of trouble. What kind of trouble are we talking about?"

"Whatever kind you dream up, of course. But Trouble is the name of Ram's female partner. I'll need a first draft in eight weeks if we're going to be able to launch in time for Christmas. Eighty thousand words minimum."

"How many of these Ram Johnson books am I on the hook for?"

"Only twelve."

"Twelve?"

"Relax, Mr. Dupree. You've got three years to write them."

"Shit."

"Problem?"

"I guess I should have read the contract, huh?"

"As I said earlier, you could take all the time you wanted to discuss it with your lawyer. Unfortunately, at this point, I'm afraid any contractual conversations will have to include mine."

"How many do you have working for you?"

"Lawyers? About fifty."

"Fifty?"

"Yes. You know, Coco is correct when she says that I hate authors. I find them cloying and far too self-absorbed. But for some reason, I do find being surrounded by lawyers somewhat comforting."

She led him by the arm towards the door.

"Come, Mr. Dupree. Let's have lunch. I believe we're serving turkey."

24

*E*ither watched Coco sleep, snoring on top of the covers, her hair splayed in about six different directions. He switched the light off and closed the door, then sat down in the living room, planning to order room service and watch football. As he studied the menu, he heard a knock on the door. He tossed the menu on the couch and discovered Coco's mother waiting, hands on hips.

"Hey," Either said, surprised.

"Nice to see you, Mr. Ore. May I come in?"

"Sure," Either said, stepping back holding the door open. "Coco's sleeping."

"I'm not surprised. How many martinis did she have?"

"Shit, I can't remember. I kinda lost count."

"Of course you did," she said, placing her purse on a table and sitting down on the couch. She draped a leg across her knee, showing, Either thought, a lot of thigh for a woman her age. But still, he noted, great thighs.

"I was just about to order a cheeseburger and fries from room service. You hungry?"

"Cheeseburger? I guess that confirms my suspicions, Mr. Ore."

"About what?"

"About your being a philistine."

"Philly? Nah, I'm originally from L.A."

She smiled and shook her head, then lit a cigarette and glanced around the suite.

"Are you comfortable here?"

"Here? What's not to like, right? And thanks, by the way. Coco mentioned you're paying for it."

186

"Yes, indeed. My daughter can be a tough negotiator when she sets her mind to it."

"Negotiator? I just call her fucking stubborn."

She laughed and blew smoke up at the ceiling.

"She did say that you had the ability to make her laugh." She looked at Either and held his eyes. "I've always wondered what that would feel like."

"Yeah, well, that's shit…uh, sorry, stuff for the two of you to work out." Either reached for the phone. "So, you hungry?"

"I guess I could eat a bit. A Grey Goose martini, please. Two olives."

"You got it."

Either placed the order and sat down in a chair across from her.

"I'd like to ask you about my daughter, Mr. Ore."

"Sure."

She continued looking at him, then stared off into the distance and said, "How is she doing?"

"Coco? I guess that's for her to say. But if you ask me, she's doing great."

"Really? I'm not referring to whatever arrangement the two of you have going on."

"Arrangement?"

"Yes. Please don't be coy with me, Mr. Ore."

"I don't do coy."

"I see," she said, lighting a fresh cigarette. "Then let me try a more direct approach."

"Knock yourself out."

"How long have you been sleeping with my daughter?"

"I've never slept with her. Not that I haven't tried."

"Really?"

"Mrs. Kinsley, can you say that without making it sound like I'm a three-year old? What is it with you two? *Really?* Somebody train you to say it like that?"

"I'm sorry, Mr. Ore. But if you aren't sleeping together, as you might say, what's the deal?"

"We're just friends. The Professor and I met her on the tour, and she just kinda joined up and came along for the ride."

"My daughter never does anything without a specific objective in mind. And I should know, since that is one thing she definitely got from her me."

"Like I said, Mrs. Kinsley, that shit is for the two of you to work out. It's none of my business. And anybody who tried to insert himself between the two of you would just be asking for trouble."

"You're probably right about that, Mr. Ore." She stretched her arms out, leaned back into the couch and yawned. "I'm tired."

"You've had a big day."

She smiled and nodded. "Yes, I've had a very big day. And most of the credit goes to your Mr. Dupree."

"He ain't mine. Not anymore. He's all yours."

"You aren't interested in continuing as his manager?"

"You offering me a job?"

"As his manager? Absolutely not. I've already assigned two of my staff to handle that particular challenge. But if you were interested, I'm sure I could find a place for you somewhere."

"Working for you?"

"Yes."

"No fucking way. Sorry…excuse the language."

"Your language is not a problem, Mr. Ore. It's just a word. So you have no interest in a job?"

"I'm not really a nine-to-five kind of guy."

"My staff wishes they could work nine-to-five," she said, laughing, reaching for her pack of cigarettes.

"There you go," Either said. "Kinda proves my point."

"So what are you plans?"

"That's a really good question. And now that it looks like I'm out of a job, I guess I'll have to start thinking about it."

"Are you one of those 'don't worry, something will turn up' kind of men?"

"I don't know about that…but something always does seem to turn up for me. I pay attention, keep my eyes open for opportunities that might be interesting."

"I see. And will your plans include my daughter?"

"Mrs. Kinsley, you and I both know that whatever she decides to do will be her decision. Coco is open to suggestion, but I learned pretty early on dealing with her, you better phrase it in the form of a question."

"Yes, that is so true," she said, smiling. "You're very…intuitive, Mr. Ore. I can see why Coco is so fond of you."

"Yeah," Either said, picking imaginary lint off his sweatshirt. "Just not fond enough."

Either climbed out of his chair when he heard the knock. He opened the door for the waiter who entered carrying a tray. Either pointed to the table, watched the waiter arrange the food and drink, then signed the slip. He handed her the martini and carried his plate back to the chair.

"You want a bite?" he said, holding up his cheeseburger.

"No, thanks," she said, taking a sip of her see-through. "The olives will be more than enough."

"You should eat more," Either said through a mouthful of burger.

"So everyone keeps telling me."

"It's really good. But for twenty-two bucks, it oughta be, right?"

She nodded and drained her martini in one gulp. She wiped her mouth and stood.

"I need to get to another appointment." She held up a hand. "No, don't get up. Enjoy your cheeseburger."

Making it sound like he was scarfing down pond scum.

"Before I forget," she said, "I'd like to invite you and Coco to a birthday party I'm having tomorrow night at my house."

"Birthday party?" Either said, swallowing, wiping his mouth with a napkin, drinking his beer. He felt her studying

189

him, like he was going to spit food all over the place, maybe spill beer on the carpet.

"Yes. One of my neighbors, Georgia Roberts, a wonderful woman I've known for years, is turning ninety-three."

"Ninety-three. That's a good run," Either said, attacking the burger.

"Yes, and she continues to be sharp as a tack. She never shuts up, but her stories are always entertaining."

"Well, at that age, I imagine she's got a lot of stories to tell."

"Yes. She has all sorts of stories about herself when she was young and beautiful, about travelling the world, and a collection of tedious stories about her family…especially her grandson, the FBI agent with some rather nasty anger management issues."

Either, about to stuff an onion ring in his mouth, paused. "FBI, huh?"

"Yes. Unfortunately, I'm sure he'll be there."

"Can't wait to meet him."

"Why? He's an officious prick."

"Aren't they all?"

"Exactly."

"What time should we be there?"

"Any time after eight. Our Mr. Dupree will be doing a special reading."

"The old lady's a fan of romance novels, huh?"

"God, no," she said, smiling. "She hates them. It's just my way of having a little fun with her on her birthday."

"And it gives you a chance to take the Professor's ego down a peg or two at the same time," Either said.

"Very good, Mr. Ore," she said, staring at him. "Very good indeed."

"I have my moments," Either said, beating back a burp.

"As I'm sure you know all too well, Mr. Dupree is very good with his fans and is obviously comfortable speaking to large crowds, but I'm afraid his ego could create some problems if it isn't managed carefully."

"Not to mention how fucking annoying he can be."

"Yes, there is that as well."

"I'll check with Coco."

"A wise choice, Mr. Ore." She headed for the door then paused and turned back. "I'm glad I dropped by. It's been…let's see. What's the word I'm looking for?"

"Enlightening?"

She flashed the crocodile smile.

"Let's go with tolerable, shall we?"

Either shrugged in her general direction then refocused on his cheeseburger.

"Whatever you say, Mrs. Kinsley."

"I think we're going to get along just fine, Mr. Ore."

25

*C*asper finished gawking at the view and stepped back inside the suite, still in awe, and doing his best not to show how pissed off he was that Either was living in luxury and enjoying the company of Coco, while he was stuck in some three-star high rise monstrosity out near Venice Beach that smelled like coconut oil and stale beer.

"Did I hear you say that *she's* paying for this place?"

"Yeah. Nice, huh?"

"It's okay, I guess."

Either snorted and grabbed two beers from the minibar. He handed one to Casper, slid the balcony door closed, and sat down across from him. Casper examined the label on the bottle, decided it was worthy of consumption, and took a drink. He grimaced and shifted in his chair.

"I think I tweaked my back yesterday when I tossed Larry off the stage."

"Yeah, you put on quite the show. Congratulations. You got exactly what you wanted. You're a star."

"I guess it would be disingenuous for me to say that the additional exposure and marketing machine support inherent in the terms of the contract weren't appealing."

"Man, in six months no normal person is going to understand a fucking word you're saying, Professor."

"Don't start, Either. Please. Not today." He exhaled loudly and stared up at the ceiling. "I think I signed a bad deal."

"You just couldn't help yourself. Coco calls it one of your signature character flaws. Hey, look on the bright side. It's only three years. You can do that standing on your head."

"Three years inside might start looking pretty good by the time this contract expires."

"Boo-fucking-hoo. You poor baby."

"But she's going to keep the Endless Tour going. Three more years on that damn bus."

"Winnebago."

"We were only on the road for a couple of months, and it was already starting to get old."

Either sank a little deeper into his chair, smiling and staring off into the distance.

"Yeah, but we had a hell of a good time, huh?"

"Yeah, we sure did," Casper said, smiling. "Maybe I can wear her down. You know, get her to change her mind."

"Professor, you'd have a better chance getting a shark to stop eating fish."

"Well, shark would be the appropriate metaphor." He exhaled again and sighed; almost a whimper. "And I'm sure that by now you and Coco are…getting horizontal."

"Yeah, sure. Two, maybe three times a day."

"Shit," Casper said. "How is it?"

"Easy to imagine, impossible to actually describe."

"You're a lucky guy. Where is Coco?"

"She's out shopping. Said it would be sacrilegious to be staying on Rodeo Drive and not pay homage to the Gods of Beverly Hills. I thought you and I could use the time to discuss a couple of business items."

"Such as?"

"First, we need to talk about the birthday party you're doing a reading at tonight."

"Oh, you heard about that? Are you coming?"

"Kinda."

"I'm not following, Either."

"Do you know whose birthday it is?"

"No, just that it's one of her neighbors turning ninety-three. That's a good run, huh?"

"Yeah. I'd be happy with that."

"Me too. Apparently she's a big fan of romance novels."

"Is that right?"

"Yeah. I figure I'll find a nice juicy section from one of my books, I'm not sure which one yet, and play it up. You know, make it nice and sexy. Give the old girl a little thrill."

"I wish I could be there to see that. Anyway, the birthday girl's name is Georgia Roberts."

"Is that supposed to mean something to me?"

"Probably not until I mention the fact that she has a grandson who works for the FBI."

"FBI? Shit. Agent Roberts is her grandson?"

"Yes, that would appear to be the case."

Casper stood and began pacing the living room.

"You realize that this raises a whole bunch of questions, don't you?"

"I do."

"How long have they been neighbors?"

"About forty years."

"So, how logical would it be to assume that Coco has met our Agent Roberts before?"

"I would say very logical."

"And yet she somehow failed to mention it."

"Exactly."

"Think it's a coincidence?" Casper said, picking up the pace of his pacing.

"Maybe…but doubtful."

"Have you confronted her about it yet?"

"No. I haven't said a word. I wanted to talk with you first. Sit down. You're making me nervous."

Casper sat back down on the couch, lit a cigarette, and tossed the pack to Either.

"I'm trying to remember," Either said, blowing smoke, "if she was around the day Agent Roberts came into the bookstore."

"Try remembering harder. This might be rather important."

"Don't rush me. Let's see…I was sitting at a table having coffee when he showed up, starting trying to mess with my head and then…yeah, I got it. She was talking with you over in the area where you were going to be doing your signing. And he definitely asked me who she was."

"Maybe he just didn't recognize her," Casper said.

"Right. Because she's so easy to forget once you've seen her."

"Yeah. But why would he lie or play dumb about that?"

"Don't know. Right now, I'm more interested in why she'd do it."

"But she was the one who came up with the idea to set up that meth head to get him off our trail."

"Yeah. I've been wondering about that myself."

"And?"

"And I think she was definitely trying to help us out and prove that she belonged. You know, deserved to be a partner in our thing."

"Yeah, I can see that."

"It makes sense. But I can't get the idea out of my head that, although she was doing everything she could to get him off our trail, for some reason she was doing it to get him off *hers*."

"Maybe she was just embarrassed to admit that she knew him."

"Well, he is a total asshole."

"You never told me exactly what happened with him."

"Agent Roberts? I'm still not sure what I did to set him off. One summer about seven years ago, we were on the same softball team here in L.A."

"You played softball?"

"Yeah. I wasn't any good in the field, but I could hit. And run like hell."

"Well, by then, you'd probably had years of practice."

"Yeah," Either said, laughing. "And before a game one night he came up to me and started screaming at me how I'd stolen some valuable family heirloom and if I didn't give it back he'd be *haunting my dreams*."

"A little clichéd, but not bad."

"Just kept screaming at me. 'Heirloom. It's a family heirloom.' Then the fucking guy started beating me with a bat. Ended up spending three weeks in the hospital."

"Jesus. What happened to him?"

"I heard he got a major suspension, got pulled off all his cases, got sent to anger management class."

"So what was this heirloom?"

"I don't have a clue. The guy never said."

"This whole thing is weird. How do you want to handle it?"

"I'm not sure how to play it with Coco yet. But I sure have an idea on how to handle Agent Roberts. I'm gonna need your help."

"To do what?"

"Before your reading tonight at the birthday party, I need you to head down to Grandma's house and disable the security system."

"Jesus, Either, I don't know."

"It's not up for debate, Professor. Consider it our swan song. One last job for old times' sake."

"I'd really rather not get involved."

"I don't give a shit, Professor. If Agent Roberts is so fond of heirlooms, I'll give him something to remember."

"Either, you know bad things happen in this business when you start doing things for revenge."

"Like I said, Professor. This isn't up for debate. I need you to head over there and turn the system off after you see her leave the house. Look, it'll be dark by then and it'll take you and your throbbing manhood two minutes."

Casper sighed, then nodded.

"Okay. But then that's it. I'm done stealing."

"Fair enough. Next, we need to discuss the several million dollars in diamonds and gold tucked behind the refrigerator."

"What about it?"

"I was thinking you wouldn't mind if I took it."

"Did you now?" Casper sat back, rested a leg over his knee and stared at Either. "Why on earth would you think that?"

"Because it's the right thing to do. It's only fair."

"I think you're the one who's been smelling too many diesel fumes, Either. Are you out of your fucking mind?"

"Probably. But that's beside the point at the moment. Let's think this through."

"Dazzle me."

"Since I was the one who tracked you down in the first place and put together the whole plan for the tour and our…let's call it our moonlighting adventure, it's only logical to infer that I'm actually the one who *discovered* you."

"Logical to infer? Am I talking to you, Either, or am I talking to Coco?"

"Yeah, we've discussed it. And we think it's only fair."

"You gonna split it with her? Jesus, Either, she doesn't need *money*. Years of intensive therapy maybe. But not money. Her mother's loaded. By now, Coco probably is too."

"That's not the point. Look, I don't know if I'm gonna give her a cut or not. But she did do a lot of work on it."

"So did I, Either. I worked my ass off."

"Relax, Professor. I figured you might not like the idea the first time you heard it."

"At least you got that much right."

"Look at it this way. As the person who put the whole thing together, as your business manager, a good case could be made that I'm owed a nice chunk of that advance you just got plus a percentage of your royalties. Both for what you've sold the past few months as well as what you're going to sell over the next three years. Without me and Coco you would never have gotten within a hundred miles of Kinsley Publishing."

"Maybe."

Either laughed and grabbed two more beers from the fridge.

"How much do you think you'll get from your buddy, Amir?"

"Hard to say until we get all the diamonds under some good light, but I'm guessing at least a couple million."

197

"Split three ways, that would be around six, seven hundred thousand for each of us."

"Sounds about right."

"That's a lot of money to leave on the table, Either."

"Yeah, it is. But if the next three years go off as planned, that'll be chump change to the new Bad Boy of Romance. Plus, you'll have peace of mind knowing that I won't be hanging around tracking your progress and expecting a piece of every book you sell."

"You'd really do that?"

"Can you really afford to take that risk? Professor, you gotta understand that this is my best shot to get out, be able to kick back, maybe do something different with my life."

"Really?"

"Do I sound like I'm fucking joking?"

"Something different?"

"Why not?"

"Like what?"

"Who knows?"

"With her?"

"Why not?"

"Just ride off into the sunset?"

"Exactly."

"Don't you worry that she's setting you up?"

"Only when I let myself think about it."

Casper removed his glasses and rubbed his forehead.

"So what do I get out of the deal?"

"My ongoing and total silence."

Either and Casper stared at each other in silence, studying one another. Either thought back, remembering what they'd managed to pull off just by agreeing to work together as partners. Good solid memories, stories he'd be calling up for years, maybe even telling someone assuming he ever found somebody he could trust. Bragging about how they'd planned and executed each job to perfection. Images of herringbone and tortoise shell overlapped and mingled with memories of acetylene torches hot enough to crisp the tips of your fingers, tight-lipped expressions caused by wrestling with the Winnebago down long stretches of windy highways. Arguing with the Professor, calling him Fuckwit - sometimes even meaning it. Living life on the road, the best time of his life that might never repeat, everything probably downhill from this point forward. Sobering news softened by the promise of cash, mitigated by the possibility of her. Either smiled now, a small smile tampered by the realization that whatever he and the Professor might call their adventure at some point down the road, one thing was certain.

It was over.

"Okay," Casper said. "Take it. It's all yours."

"Thanks, Professor."

Casper extended a hand.

"Nice working with you."

26

"**O**h, I see," Coco's mother said. "Silly me, I thought you had dropped by to help me get ready for the party."

"Help *you*, Mother?" Coco said, glancing around the house. "There must be thirty people here."

"Yes, well, it's the thought that would have counted, darling. Coffee, maybe something a bit stronger?"

"God, yes," Coco said, heading into the kitchen. She sat down at a massive granite island, now surrounded by copper pots and pans of all sizes hanging on hooks.

"Martini?" her mother said, holding up a bottle of Grey Goose.

"No, thanks," Coco said, shaking her head. "I think I'm going to be off the see-throughs for a while. You still make a great Bloody Mary?"

"It's one of my singular talents," she said, collecting ingredients. "So, darling, what on earth possessed you to just pop in announced?"

"Don't worry, Mother. I won't be making a habit of it."

"You're always welcome here, Coco. You know that," she said, focused on getting the wrapper off a bottle of Worcestershire sauce. "Damn," she said, now struggling. "Fucking over packaging. If I wrapped books this way, nobody would ever read."

"Nobody reads now," Coco said.

"My accountants would beg to differ with you, darling," she said, tearing away the wrapping. "Hah, take that, you bastard." She shook the bottle and added a healthy dash of Worcestershire to a pitcher, squeezed the juice of half a lemon and lime, splashed hot sauce, sprinkled celery salt and lots of pepper, then stirred. She poured two large glasses, added

200

skewers of olives and celery stalks then slid one of the glasses in Coco's direction. Both took sips and nibbled olives.

"I don't think I've ever seen you work that hard in the kitchen, Mother."

"So that's why you dropped by? For another round of mommy-bashing? You really need to get over it and start focusing on all the things I did give you."

"Like what?"

"Well," she said, "for starters, how about incredible strength and independence that tells the world not to screw with you. And striking looks…you certainly didn't get those from your father."

"Let's not bring him into this, okay?"

"Fine. And how about your sense of style? That is a gorgeous top."

"Thanks. I picked it up this morning."

"Rodeo?"

"Of course. You were buying."

Coco raised her glass in mock-salute.

"There, right there," she said, pointing at the glass. "That *edge*. Who do you think you got that from? But I guess I never considered the possibility you'd use it on me."

Coco took a sip, then lit a cigarette. She slid the pack across the island, and her mother lit one of her own. Smoking in silence, they maintained eye contact.

"What did you always say?" Coco said. "These are the ultimate calorie avoiders?"

"Absolutely. They save me at least a thousand a day."

"Still think they're worth the risk?"

"Who knows? But if they do end up killing me, I'll go out gorgeous, in a slimming casket with people shedding tears about how I was taken away far too early. Call me crazy, but I'll take that over old and fat any day."

"I need a favor, Mother."

"Really?"

"Yeah."

"Apart from your allowance being deposited by the first of the month, I thought you didn't need anything from me."

"Don't worry. I won't be making a habit of it."

Coco refilled both glasses and sat back in her chair.

"Well, don't keep me waiting, darling. What's the favor?"

"I need you to introduce me to John Wilson."

"The guy who owns Flagstone Publishing?"

"Yes."

"Wow," she said, stirring her Bloody Mary with a celery stalk. "Darling, you could have given me a million guesses and I wouldn't have gotten it. Why on earth do you want to meet him? He's happily married with a zillion kids."

"He publishes crime books."

"Yes, dear. I'm aware of that. What with my being in the publishing industry and all."

"Jesus. Let one go once in a while, Mother."

"Sorry. Please continue."

"I have an idea for a book."

"Really?"

"Do I look like I'm joking?"

"A crime book?"

"Yes."

"You want to write a book about crime?"

"Yes. It's something I've always wanted to do," Coco said, raising her hand, cutting her mother off before she could respond. "And if you say 'Really?' I'm going to punch you right in the nose."

"Why now?"

"It's been coming on ever since I joined those two on that book tour."

"Ah, yes, the Tour. And that really was all Mr. Ore's idea?"

"Yeah, it was."

"It's pure genius. To look at him, you wouldn't think he had it in him."

"No. Not at first. But he tends to surprise you when you least expect it."

"I guess I can see that." She took a sip of Bloody Mary. "But he's not for you, darling."

"I know," Coco said, beating back a wave of emotion. "It was strange watching the Professor do those signings. He'd be reading some piece of shit schlock and he'd just pull the audience in, get them in the palm of his hand and be able to take them anywhere he wanted. I realized that I'd like to be able to do the same thing."

"You're already able to do that, darling."

"Yeah, I guess. But I'd like to be able to do it because of something I've done, not because of whose birth canal I popped out of."

"Now there's an image," she said. "It's probably a good idea for you to stick with crime, darling. I don't think you have much of a future in romance."

"We're still talking about books, right?"

Her mother laughed. Coco eventually joined in.

"What was it like on the bus with those two? I'm guessing it was horrible, but that's just me projecting."

Coco blew smoke up into the overhead fan and gave the question some thought. "Actually, it was great. Like an extended school trip with no supervisors."

"And with two adolescent boys vying for your love and affection."

"Not to mention my scant lavenders."

"What?"

"Nothing. Long story."

"All the good ones are, dear. So, since you rebuffed Mr. Ore's attempts, can I assume that Mr. Dupree had more success?"

"Either told you, huh?"

"He inferred as much last night. Personally, I find him much more interesting than that preening fool, but you always did seem to have a weakness for the self-absorbed."

"It's definitely a flaw, yes."

Coco proceeded to tell the story about how close she had come with Casper until his unfortunate mistake. Her mother exploded with laughter, choked on an olive, and endured a coughing fit until she recovered.

"Gwen? Who the hell is Gwen?"

"No idea. And he swears he doesn't either."

"You didn't give him another chance, did you?"

"Absolutely not."

"Good girl. So about this book…what's the hook?"

"The bad guys win."

"So it's non-fiction?"

Coco laughed, enjoying her mothers' company for the first time since…damn, when was the last?

"It's a crime novel. I got the idea one day on the tour when I walked past a jewelry store in the mall where the Professor was doing a signing. It's about an author doing a book tour and using it as a front to hide the fact that she's knocking off jewelry stores."

Coco caught the raised eyebrow her mother was giving her.

"She? Your main character is female?"

"Relax, Mother. It's fiction."

"If you say so, darling."

"Don't worry, Mother. Everything's under control. So what do you think?"

"I think Flagstone will snap it up. And if they don't, I'll talk with John."

"No, please don't do that. At least not until I ask you to."

"Okay. It's your call."

"The book's about someone trying to come to terms with their dark side. On the one hand, a successful author enjoying fame and the adulation of her fans while, on the other, fighting personal demons that threaten to destroy her entire life."

Her mother listened closely, nodding.

"Yeah. Nice," she said. "Add a love angle, clean up some of the bad language I know you're going to use, and I'll publish the fucking thing."

"Not a chance, Mother."

"It was worth a shot. You got a title?"

"Yeah. I'm gonna call it…Either Or."

Her mother drained her glass, and stood.

"I need to check on how things are going outside. You're still coming, right?"

"Eight o'clock. I'm going to head upstairs and grab a sweater. It's supposed to be cold tonight. I'm assuming all my stuff is still there."

"Nothing's been touched, dear. I haven't gone in your room in years. Remember? I'm not allowed in there."

Her mother winked and gave her a small wave before heading outside through the French doors. Coco finished her drink, washed both glasses, then headed upstairs.

Stepping inside her room was like stepping back in time-a clumsy metaphor the Professor overworked and reused, but it worked here: Posters, stuffed animals, and other remnants of a childhood spent hiding in this room, her sanctuary from her mother and life in general.

So many memories. So many questions.

Why was happiness impossible?

Why was time moving so slowly?

Most often, she wondered when she'd be old enough to get the hell out of here and not have to worry about someone coming after her to bring her back?

Memories.

Fuck it.

Better to just find it and get the hell out of here before her brain cramped.

Coco opened a drawer and tossed a thick sweater on the bed. She headed to her closet, a massive enclosure that ran the length of the room. She turned the light on and ran her hand along the expanse of blouses, skirts and formal wear hung neatly. Boxes of shoes, some unopened, spilled on the floor. She dug her way past a built-in holding the remainder of her shoe collection to a small safe installed in the wall. She punched in the combination and opened the door. She extracted a felt pouch, put the closet back in order, then walked back into the room and sat down on the bed.

She reached inside the pouch and pulled out the bracelet, examining it, really seeing it for the first time. Massive diamonds and other precious stones she'd never paid much attention to when she'd stolen it. She'd grown tired of always hearing about it from the woman down the street and her annoying grandson. How it was a priceless family heirloom, how it continued to be handed down from generation to generation. How the now Agent Roberts was next in line assuming he ever found somebody dumb enough to marry him. The old woman and her mother had laughed hard at that one. She'd felt sorry for the guy, since being laughed at by your own family *resonated* with her.

She'd stolen it because she was sick and tired of hearing about it.

And because she could.

Now, holding it seven years later, staring at it, examining her ticket to freedom in the light, she smiled and slid it back into the pouch. She tucked it inside the sweater, headed downstairs and gently closed the door behind her.

27

*C*asper removed his jacket, a new herringbone that went with his glasses, and hung it on a low hanging branch. He rolled his cuffs to mid-calf – probably not a good idea to show up for his reading with muddy pants – and scanned the outside of the house.

No floodlights; one less thing to worry about.

Locating the wiring to the alarm system; very familiar, a piece of cake to disable.

Installing the bypass.

Testing the signal.

Satisfied, he approached the house and soon found the unlocked window he was looking for.

He slid it open a few inches and waited.

Nothing.

No clicks or beeps this particular system emitted when breached.

He did hear a low rumble that gave him pause, but it didn't repeat, and he chalked it up to the wind.

He retrieved his jacket, rolled his pants down and waved to Either, who was hiding behind a large bougainvillea.

Either approached, rubbing the back of his neck, muttering and cursing under his breath.

"Can you make a little less noise?" Casper said, grimacing and rubbing his lower back.

"I hate those things. The flowers are nice, but those thorns are nasty. We all set?"

"Yeah, easy one. You could have a party in there and nobody would know. Just don't touch the alarm system and you'll be fine."

"Thanks, Professor. I owe you one."

"You gonna stop by the party after?"

"I don't think that's a good idea. Agent Roberts may be a little slow, but even he'd be able to put this one together if he happened to see me tonight."

"Okay," Casper said, shuffling his feet in the cool night air. "I guess this is where we say goodbye, right?"

"Yeah, I guess so," Either said. "Take care of yourself, man. And try not to let her get her hooks into you too deep."

"Too late for that I'm afraid. I'd give you the same advice, but you're way past that point too."

"Yeah. All right. I'm off," Either said, starting to walk away, but then stopping. "But before I go, there's something I need to do. Something I've wanted to do for a long time."

Either inched closer and grabbed Casper's head and tousled his hair. Casper slapped his hands away and glared at him.

"You're such a dumbass, Either."

"See you later, Fuckwit."

**

Coco, still nursing a hangover, nursed a glass of wine and surveyed the crowd. A collection of her mother's friends and neighbors, many she'd known growing up, others unfamiliar. A handful of Kinsley employees were gathered outside huddled around the fire pit, drinking, and checking their phones. Coco smiled and waved to the birthday girl; ninety-three and moving slow but not missing a trick, her eyes sparkling almost as much as the collection of diamonds on her hand, wrist and neck. She winked at Coco and gave her a small wave in return.

Casper approached, one eye on a mirror behind Coco, one hand pushing stray hairs back under the control of way too much product.

"Hello, Professor," she said, greeting him with a nod. "Are you ready for this?"

"Well," he said, glancing around, "I guess it will be okay, but doing a reading at a party might be tough. You know, noise, controlling the crowd…I think I'm going to read a selection from *Pining Through the Pines*."

"Throbbing members in the forest, lots of metaphors about how the lovers could make it work if they could only see the forest through the trees?"

"Oh, you've read it."

"Not a chance. But I'm sure they'll all be rapt."

"Yeah, me too."

Coco glanced around the room.

"You know," she whispered, "I was thinking that it might have been fun to work some book clubs into our operation."

"You mean do a signing in somebody's living room and knock off the house at the same time?"

"Yeah."

"Interesting," Casper said, giving it some thought. "That's not bad. I come in early, disable the security, and then you and I entertain the crowd while Either hits the second story. Yeah, I can see that working. Oh well, I guess it's too late now, huh?"

"For you, it certainly is."

Coco laughed and waved to her mother, who was watching them.

"I'll be fine," Casper said, also waving. "You're making too big a deal out of it."

"Keep telling yourself that," Coco said. "Is Either coming?"

"No, I don't think so."

"Where is he?"

"You don't want to know."

**

Either pulled on a pair of surgical gloves, then approached the window. He slid it open, paused to listen for any warning sounds then, hearing nothing but a low rumble he decided was the heating system kicking on, climbed through the window and closed it behind him. He waited for his eyes to adjust to the available light hoping he wouldn't need to use his flashlight.

"Okay," he whispered. "Family heirlooms. Whatever the hell they might be."

Second thoughts about being here boiled in his mind. He wondered why he'd let his anger get the best of him, revenge not being a wise motive.

Rule number one: Never make it personal.

But here he was, standing in the living room of a strange house he'd done no advance prep work on, no idea where anything was, forced to just make it up as he went along. The best way he knew of to end up doing stupid shit, like getting caught. But he headed upstairs.

**

Coco watched Agent Roberts as he followed his grandmother, hovering, trying to help her with her plate of food and cocktail. The old woman swatting his hand away, cursing under her breath, glaring at her grandson, confused and helpless and starting to see his share of the inheritance dwindling.

Agent Roberts spotted Coco and approached, seeking sanctuary.

"Family, huh?" he said. "What can you do?"

"Don't worry. You'll get your cut."

"Yeah. Hard to believe, but I'm still her favorite."

"I'm going to get another drink."

"Hang on a sec." He steered her to a quiet corner of the room. "I'm coming off suspension in a couple of days."

"Good for you."

"I'm going to need your help."

"Jesus. Really?"

"Do I sound like I'm joking?"

"No, I'm done. We had a deal."

"Yes. And the deal was that if you were able to return a certain piece of jewelry to me, then you'd be done. Do you see anything sparkling on my wrist?"

"No. What's the job?"

"Nothing you can't handle. Stop by my office next week and I'll take you through it."

Coco nodded and started to walk to the bar. He grabbed her arm, and she stopped, glaring at him.

"Where's our friend, Either?"

"I wouldn't have a clue," she said, freeing her arm. "I haven't seen him since yesterday. Actually, I think he might have taken off." She nodded in the direction of Casper, who was attempting to regale her mother and the old lady with a story. Both women, masters of polite-boredom, nodded at Casper and forced smiles. "My mother just signed him to a three-year deal."

"Poor bastard."

"Yeah. But that cuts Either out of the loop and leaves him with nothing to do. I'm guessing he's gone. He's been talking about taking a vacation."

"Where?"

"Why do you care?"

Agent Roberts shrugged.

"I just feel better when I have some idea where the little prick is."

**

Either entered the master bedroom and began examining a collection of photos and knickknacks on a long table. Again he heard the low rumble and listened closely, still not sure what to make of it. He resumed his search for heirlooms, totally lost about what might be valuable. For all he knew, he might be doing the old lady a favor by getting rid of all this dust-collecting crap. He examined the family photos, her at a young age-definitely a looker, posing in a white wedding dress next to her husband, both of them with big smiles. A couple of photos

211

of a young Agent Roberts, others of the whole extended family huddled close, making sure they all got in the shot.

Giving up on the search for heirlooms Either whispered, "What the hell, as long as I'm here." and began searching for a safe. Peeking behind mirrors and paintings hanging on the wall, he soon found what he was looking for.

Bingo.

He removed his backpack and felt inside for his torch.

**

Coco worked her way to the edge of the crowd so she could watch the Professor and still keep one eye on the party. She studied him as he cleared his throat, flipped the book open and adjusted his glasses.

Either was right; the tortoise shell was fucking annoying.

He began reading. Her mother and the old lady continued chatting and laughing, enjoying their cocktails, ignoring Casper completely, along with pretty much the rest of the crowd. Her mother glanced over to catch Coco's eye, then nodded at Casper and laughed. Coco knowing that her mother making the Professor do a reading tonight was just one more way for her to drive the nail in about who was calling the shots now.

But Coco had to give him credit. Nervous, but he hung tough, working his way through the selection. He spoke louder to be heard above the party noise, trying to set the mood with a passage about some couple reuniting in a pine forest, going for hushed-hot, but forced to shout.

Coco thought back to her one time having sex in a pine forest, something not easily forgotten. How she'd fallen for his line about how romantic it would be to make love on a soft bed of pine needles, back when she was too young and stupid to know any better. The guy she'd originally considered a real romantic was simply too fucking cheap to spring for a room. She'd ended up with pine needles stuck to her cooch and about a thousand mosquito bites on her ass. Cursing about the mosquitos and yelling at the guy to do something, the only time in her life she'd tolerated being spanked.

Sex in a pine forest.

Really, Professor?

Coco watched as the Professor finally succumbed to boozy-indifference, jumped to the end of the passage, then finished to a short golf clap. He tossed the book in the fire pit and headed for the bar.

Coco focused on Agent Roberts playing sycophant to his grandmother, who again glared at him and cursed, waving him away with the back of her hand.

She walked back inside and headed to the kitchen. She rinsed her empty wineglass and put it in the dish washer, thinking about how some habits simply refused to die.

Coco washed her hands, took one final look around, then left through the back door.

**

About to light his torch, Either paused when the low rumble got louder and transformed into a throaty growl. Either slowly placed the torch in his backpack and zipped it shut. He slid the backpack over his shoulders, staring into the darkness, afraid of discovering the owner of the growl.

Either, legs shaking, took a deep breath and shined the flashlight at a black-eyed beast showing lots of teeth. The growl intensified. Either guessed the beast didn't like what it was seeing.

At least they had something in common.

Either glanced around the room and realized the dog had probably been stalking him since he'd first climbed through the window. Either reached into the pockets of his jacket and found a couple of peanut butter crackers he'd been saving for later. Unwilling to reach his hand out, he tossed them in the general direction of the dog, who ignored them, barked once, then resumed the growl.

Either went back into his pockets. He tossed a stick of gum, a strand of red licorice, and a Vicodin to the dog. Each peace offering ignored, the dog, panting heavily, took a step closer and continued to stare into Either's eyes.

"Focused little bastard, aren't you?"

**

Agent Roberts, thoroughly pissed off about the fact that there was no pleasing the old woman, tossed back another scotch and snapped his fingers at the bartender for a refill. His phone buzzed, and he glanced down to check the number calling him. Realizing it wasn't a call but rather an alert from the app he'd gotten to monitor Tank, he launched it and reviewed the dog's vitals. Rapid breathing. Elevated heart rate. Odd, he thought, since the only thing the dog did when he was alone was sleep and snore. He studied the numbers and saw that they were continuing to rise. He closed his phone and slipped out a side door.

**

Either backed his way to the window, his only possible escape route. The dog took a couple of steps in his direction, breathing heavier but still in control, drool foaming at the side of its mouth. The growling intensified. Reaching behind him without taking his eyes off the beast, Either began to worry about bladder control.

His fingers found the latch and he gently slid the window open. Feeling the cool breeze, Either decided to go for it. In one move he turned and launched himself through the window as the dog launched itself and nipped his ankle.

Either, free falling and cursing himself for spending his entire night doing stupid shit, landed face first on the flat roof that ran along the side of the house. He rolled over onto his back and looked up at the window through watery eyes, blood

214

gushing from his broken nose. The dog, apoplectic, barked and growled, then disappeared from the window.

Either struggled to his feet and limped his way along the roof, trying to find a soft landing spot on the ground below. He continued to work his way around the narrow roof that wrapped around the first floor. Eventually it opened up above what he assumed was the garage. He stopped to catch his breath and wipe blood off his face with his jacket sleeve. He checked his ankle. It hurt like hell, but was probably, he hoped, just a bad sprain.

About to resume his search for a way off the roof, he heard the dog, growling and working his head under the partially opened window. The dog pulled its head back and used its paws to push the window further up.

"What the fuck?" Either said, paralyzed with fear but mesmerized by the dog's focus and tenacity.

Either watched the dog wiggle its way through the window then limped as fast as he could to the edge of the roof. He glanced down into the darkness, glanced back at the dog now racing across the roof, and jumped. Either landed hard and heard two snaps. First, the sound of his ankle shattering, then the unmistakable sound of a bullet being racked into the chamber of a semi-automatic pistol.

Either rolled to his knees and looked up at the gun barrel pointing at his head, then at the arm holding the gun. He saw Agent Roberts' smiling face.

"Any final requests, Either?"

"Put the fucking gun down, Agent Roberts."

"Aren't you forgetting something?"

Either flashed him that smile.

"Please?"

28

Coco took one final look at the beach outside her patio.
People arriving carried morning cocktails and books to read.
They sat in their cabanas enjoying the sun and water without
frying themselves. She closed her eyes and let the ocean breeze
wash over her, then checked her watch.

She stepped inside the suite and dialed the number.

"Hi," she said, to the voice on the other end. "It's me."

"Well, hello," Agent Roberts said. "I've been trying to get
hold of you. Where are you?"

"Cleveland."

"Sure. And I'm the president of France."

"I just thought I'd give you a call before."

"Before what?"

"You'll see," Coco said, checking her watch again.

"Hang on," Agent Roberts said, "There's somebody at the
door."

"They're right on time."

"What? Okay, okay, I'm coming…"

Coco listened to the door opening and the mumbled
conversation. Moments later, Agent Roberts was back on the
phone.

"It was two guys who looked like they worked for the
Secret Service."

"It's a high end delivery service. Very secure. I didn't feel
comfortable trusting Fed Ex with something that valuable."

"What is it?"

"Open it."

Through the phone, Coco heard cardboard ripping and the
rustling of paper.

"Son of a bitch," Agent Roberts whispered.

"Isn't that what you've been looking for?"

"I can't believe it. You got it back from him."

"Yes…I got it back to you."

"This is unbelievable. Thank you, Coco. You have no idea what this means. So, what special acts of kindness did you need to perform?"

"I just had to go to a place where I'm not comfortable and swallow hard."

"My mind is racing."

"And that's going to have to sustain you, Agent Roberts. We had a deal, right?"

Coco waited out the pause. Even now the bastard was trying to torment her.

"Yes," he said. "We've got a deal."

"No more jobs or special favors from me, right?"

"Yeah. That was the deal."

"And him too. You're going to leave him alone?"

"Apart from his upcoming trial, I don't give a shit about what happens to Either Ore."

"Good. Thank you."

"So how did you get it back?"

"Does it really matter?"

"No, I guess not. Hey, I heard you got a book deal."

"Yeah. I need something to do. We'll see how it goes."

"Romance novel?"

"Not a chance."

"I'll keep an eye out for it. And I want a signed copy. You going to write it under your name?"

"No, I'm using a pen name. I'm trying to keep a low profile about who my mother is."

"Most people would be playing that fact up to the hilt."

"Yeah, well, I guess I'm not like most people."

"No, you most certainly aren't. So what name are you gonna use?"

"Coco Notgwen."

"Not Gwen?"

"It's a long story."

"All the good ones are, right?"

"Exactly."

Her phone buzzed. She checked the number, said goodbye to Agent Roberts for what she hoped was the last time in her life, and answered the call.

"This is Gwen."

"You're never gonna let that go are you?"

"Nope. What's up?"

"I'll tell you what's up. I'm stuck on this Winnebago, probably forever, with two people your mother assigned, and they're driving me nuts."

"Why are you whispering?"

"Because *they'll* hear me. One of them is my new manager who has completely overscheduled me. The other is looking over my shoulder every day making sure I get my two thousand words written. They're a couple of overbearing wannabes. I'm telling you, Coco, I can't take it."

"Where are you?"

"Somewhere between Phoenix and Albuquerque. I've got *three* signings tonight."

"So just jump out. I hear the desert is nice this time of year."

"Coco, please talk with your mother."

"Not a chance, Professor."

"I don't think I can do this."

"But this is what you wanted. A shot at the big leagues, right?"

"Yeah, maybe. But I didn't think I'd be completely controlled and run ragged by a couple of kids with MBAs and the corporate climb on their mind."

"You poor baby," Coco said, chuckling.

"And I think your mother has promised them promotions if they successfully *manage my performance* and the next six months meet her expectations. She wouldn't do that, would she?"

"No, Professor, she wouldn't."

"Well, I'm glad to hear that."

"My mother would have promised promotion to *one* of them."

"But which one?"

"Nobody knows. Not even my mother at this point. That's part of the fun, Professor."

"Shit."

"Exactly."

"I miss our thing," he said.

"Yeah, me too. But try to look on the bright side. Maybe you can find a nice place to knock off if you ever get some downtime."

"Yeah, find one of our red-tile roof specials. But it wouldn't be the same without you and Either."

"Have you talked to him?"

"Yeah. A couple times."

"And?"

"He's still not ready to talk."

"He hates me, doesn't he?"

"Well, hate is a strong word. And it's on the opposite side of the love coin. I'd say, right now, he's trying to balance on the edge of it. Hey, that's not bad. I can probably use that."

"Focus, Professor."

"Sorry. I guess the thing he's wondering about the most is why you just took off with everything we had."

"I'm sorry."

"Hey, don't apologize to me. It wasn't my money."

"I'm just…keeping it safe for now."

"Sure, Coco. Whatever you say. So you won't talk with your mother?"

"Would you be willing to speak with Either about me?"

"Not a chance."

"Well, there you go," she said. "Take care of yourself, Professor."

"Yeah, later…"

Before he hung up, she heard,

"What? Get off my back will you? I said I'd fucking take care of it."

Coco laughed and tossed the phone on the desk. She stretched out on the bed and started making plans for the day. Three days into her stay, already in love with Grand Cayman, she sipped wine on her patio and watched the moon shine light all over the rolling surf. This was as good a place as any to get some serious writing done. Not one word yet, but lots of notes and fresh memories that would need to settle before she could formulate a coherent story.

A story about a woman who wrote books about crime and also knocked off jewelry stores in her spare time. Change the narrative enough to protect the guilty, change the names, and lose the Winnebago. Maybe give her main character her own private jet, like the one she'd chartered three days ago. Flying here after spending two days convincing Either's fence, Amir, why she deserved three million for the collection she'd removed from the Winnebago.

Amir had started off offering two and a half, his eyes bugging out at the size and quality of the haul. His eyes had almost fallen out of his head when he'd gotten a close horizontal look at her. He'd been tough to deal with, macho and dominant with strange outdated ideas about a woman's place, but great in bed and able to maintain the right amount of indifference to it being anything more than part of their negotiations. And agreeing to sleep with him had been the right negotiating strategy, certainly better than accepting his offer to go out clubbing, what with the L.A. traffic being the absolute nightmare it was.

She headed out to the patio, poured a cup of coffee, and tore the cellophane off a fresh pack of cigarettes. She leaned her head back and exhaled smoke, the breeze whisking it away.

Yeah, she decided, this was the place.

She'd need to call that real estate agent on the house she'd seen, only a couple of miles away and still beachfront. Basically a bungalow that needed work, but nothing major, with an asking price of two and a half million she knew she could get it for two with a cash offer.

A decent security system, but nothing they couldn't handle.

She smiled at the thought and sipped her coffee.

Either.

Thinking about him a lot the past few days, which only made sense, given the freshness of their history. That, plus the fact that she'd walked off with the entire three million, most of which was rightfully his.

Sorry, Either.

Hoping he wasn't taking things too personally, what with him suffering a temporary, but still major, setback.

Hoping he understood that their adventure had to play out this way.

At least for Round One.

Hoping his ankle was okay, but knowing he'd find his feet, bounce back and probably come looking for her.

And his money.

Maybe the best plan was to get settled in and figure out a way to let him know where she was, get him down here in the sand and sun. She could just hand him his share of the three million to take the wind out of his sail, settle him down, and try to have the conversation using her best voice on him without him getting all doe-eyed and twitchy in the process. Yeah, just hand him his share when he showed up.

That's what she'd do.

Probably.

Maybe.

Or…maybe just wait and see what happened when he finally tracked her down, hell-bent and probably with a serious case of revenge on his mind.

Revenge on His Mind.

Might be a good title. Find a new angle, a fresh narrative that could be the basis for a sequel, their story not yet fully played out. Maybe finally agreeing to let him get her out of her scant lavenders, even with the fallout that might create.

Wondering now if he'd even still be interested in getting her horizontal. Horizontal and *still alive* that is. He would, even if only out of spite.

Perhaps her thinking, fucked up as it was, was a sign of madness.

What did he fuck like when he was mad?

But wasn't he the one who'd made the decision to go another round with Agent Roberts? He couldn't blame her for that, could he? And if he hadn't gone off half-cocked, he could have been here with her right now.

Probably.

Maybe.

Maybe she would have to let him get her horizontal at least once, just to find out what was really on his mind.

Thinking a lot.

Too much thinking.

Maybe finally take her mother's advice and see if she could find a good therapist down here, someone to confide in about why it was so important for the bad girl to win one once in a while.

Really?

Yeah, there was no doubt about that.

At some point she'd have to talk with somebody.

Either that, or maybe the writing would kick in and serve as the perfect form of therapy.

Just write it all down, make peace with Either, and see where everything led from there.

Yeah, that's what she'd do.

Exactly.

29

*E*ither got arrested, got a good lawyer, got a year.

Broke his ankle, broke his nose, then got his heart broken.

Breaking and entry, attempted robbery, trespassing, vagrancy, plus a couple of other bogus charges that Agent Roberts had tried to pull from the dusty archives of crimes still on the books, determined to put Either away for a long time. In the end, the only thing that could be proved was that someone had bypassed the security system, and Either had been caught limping around the garage roof, trying to escape from a frothy, rabid Rottweiler named Tank.

Agent Roberts interrupted with an occasional protest until the judge finally told him to sit his ass back down and keep his mouth shut. Listening to the lawyers and the judge discuss his situation, negotiating his punishment like they were trying to finalize a deal on a used car, Either had been hopeful. But his prior conviction had been enough to convince the judge that a year as the guest of the state of California might be the best thing for Mr. Either Ore.

Now three months in, he'd pretty much settled into life in this medium-security establishment, not the low security prison he should have been put in all. Agent Roberts had been such a pain in the ass, arguing about how Either was a chronic offender and a low-life, life-long criminal. Plus, all the low security joints were filled up with white collar criminals and guys caught selling weed.

All in all, not a bad bunch in here. A lot of guys who definitely had an edge, but not the dangerous type you'd have to worry about sticking you in the ribs with a homemade shank. As long as you minded your own business. Either decided early on not to make any waves with the staff or inmates. He did everything he was asked, within reason, not willing to risk fucking up and having an extra six months or year thrown at him.

Either made friends. One guy was running a B&E operation right out of his cell, pulling down a couple hundred grand a year, not breaking a sweat. The guy had needed to find a new fence, though. Either'd turned him onto Amir, who was still apologizing for doing the deal with Coco; how she'd told him she was there on his behalf, how he would have never given her three million if he had only known the real story. The apology had worked until Amir pissed him off by providing all the details about his two days with Coco.

Either, still wearing a soft cast on his broken ankle that seemed to be healing fine, shuffled to a quiet hallway out of sight of the video monitors and staff. He pulled out a smartphone he'd borrowed from his B&E colleague and punched in the Professor's number. He waited until it went to voice mail – the man was impossible to reach these days – and left a short message. He headed back up the hall, handed the phone back to its owner, and entered the common room.

It was pretty much empty. Either was grateful for the quiet since the room with its linoleum floor, pool table and Ping-Pong could get loud. Inmates cursing at each other, throwing paddles, betting bottles of whiskey, chocolate and smartphones; the replacement for cigarettes as the new mother lode of prison contraband.

Either nodded to the guy reading a book on the couch and grabbed the remote. He flipped on the TV and cursed himself for forgetting his show had come on at the top of the hour. *House Hunters International*. Cayman Islands. Coming out of commercial to the summary of all three properties, each one pretty nice, none of them below a couple million, deciding which one he'd choose. He felt good when the couple picked the same one, showing good taste and a sense of style.

Looking at the white beach right off the front lawn.

Yeah, he thought, life could be good if you let it.

Watching the happy couple being interviewed six months later, smiling and laughing about how it had been the best thing they'd ever done, deciding that the Caymans might not be a bad place to land after he walked out of here. The show ended, followed by commercials, then right into some entertainment interview show. Either, about to turn it off since he'd seen the Professor on the same show a month ago and swore he'd never watch it again, did a double take when the host mentioned the name of her guest.

Coco NotGwen?

Either had to give her credit. The woman certainly had style and a sense of humor, not to mention a very long memory.

He focused on the screen and watched the camera zoom in on the long-necked vision in a lavender blouse. Her long legs on display in a short skirt, her hair blonder from either a dye job or from spending a lot of time in the sun. Laughing with the host, talking about her new…what? Book deal?

"You gotta be fucking kidding me," Either said to the TV.

Either turned the volume up.

"Hey."

Either ignored the voice from the couch and listened to her talking about how the idea just came to her, launching into a long story and sounding way too much like the Professor, chatting away about how the book was about choices, the choice between good and evil, and how she was going to call it *Either Or*.

"Hey. I'm talking to you."

Either did a half-turn and flashed that smile at the guy on the couch.

"Relax, Cowboy."

"Turn the goddamn TV down."

Either turned all the way around to face the guy stretched out on the couch, and saw the photo of the guy on the back of the book. That goofy smile and those annoying tortoise shell glasses. Either shook his head. No escaping his past, even locked up in here.

He turned back to the TV and studied her. Relaxed, smiling, and using that voice to seduce everybody who might be watching, flipping her hair back with a gentle brush of her hand, then using it to smooth out her skirt that was starting to work its way up her thigh.

In short, tormenting him.

Giving him something to think about.

But was it possible for him to think of anything about her and not get even more pissed off than he already was?

There must be something.

Scant lavenders?

Exactly.

"Hey, Dumbass. I said turn that fucking thing down. I'm trying to read here."

If you enjoyed *Either Ore*, be sure to check out B.R. Snow's Damaged Po$$e series. Here's a look at *American Midnight*, the first book in this popular series.

**

Doc White wakes up in a Las Vegas hotel suite a very confused man with a massive tequila hangover. As he reflects on the previous day's events that included his wife walking out on him and with their joint savings, the return of the voice in his head, his subsequent loss of another $150,000 at the blackjack tables, and then waking up next to a total stranger, Doc's already damaged life has taken another serious dip downward. In order to pay off his new debt, Doc is forced to do something he vowed years ago never to do again; take a corporate job. Doc's new boss, an octogenarian Chinese casino owner with a taste for curling and political intrigue, along with the return of an old love help to reenergize Doc as he tries to rebuild his life in Sin City. At a major crossroads, Doc draws on the expertise of Merlin, his coke-addled, phobic colleague from a prior life and Summerman, a part-time ghost who is certain he can help Doc deal with the voice in his head. By the time this initial installment in B.R. Snow's Damaged Posse series is wrapped up, Doc, Merlin, and Summerman have joined forces and are armed and ready to wreak havoc on the bad guys as well as themselves.

Chapter 1

I woke at five with an empty heart and a head full of tequila. Two hours of sleep had no effect on my internal clock that over the years had developed its own on-off switch. I did maintain some control over when to turn it off; but the on-switch flipped at five.

I swayed as I got out of bed, amazed I had regained consciousness. Knowing all too well that gambling and drinking were a deadly combination, I cursed my stupidity. I had certainly planned on getting drunk, but only after winning a few grand at blackjack. Some plans were meant to be broken. This wasn't one of them.

I shuffled across the suite. A mirror beckoned but I couldn't bring myself to look. Not yet anyway.

Last night started to come back.

Stacks of chips. Green, black, purple. How much had it been? Seventy, maybe eighty thousand? Certainly not major league, but big for me.

The woman in the red dress. Perched against my right shoulder, nuzzling my neck, whispering in my ear. Her words lost in casino noise and my lack of focus on what she was saying. But I remembered the nuzzling.

I remembered my cockiness too. The early evening success that followed the utter despair of the day.

And the booze. Alcohol was a regular companion, but pounding tequila shooters at the blackjack table was incomprehensible.

And unforgivable.

Don't drink and gamble, the voice had warned.

Absent for the past several weeks, the voice had returned yesterday and refused to leave.

From the corner of my eye, the mirror beckoned. I moved forward cautiously and scanned the dresser top where my clothes and belongings were heaped.

No chips. That was probably bad news.

Keys, wallet, cigarettes, cell phone, watch…something was missing. Silently, I repeated the list. Keys, wallet, cigarettes, cell phone, watch…wedding ring. Wedding ring. In a flood of emotions too powerful for a half-drunk, hung-over man old enough to know better, I remembered why I came to Vegas in the first place.

Yesterday morning my wife of only a year and a half had announced as I stepped naked from the shower she was leaving. And she left. For Greece. Something about finding a real man, a man bronzed by the sun, to love her and treat her like the lady she was. Or did she say could be? I couldn't remember her exact words because at the time I was busy getting soap out of my ears. I did remember my response.

"Leaving? What a good idea."

At least it had been until I called the bank thirty minutes later to check the status of our joint account. The automated voice on the end of the line was far too unemotional in announcing the account's current balance was $1. That is, it was $1 after my Greek-god-seeking, soon to be ex-wife had withdrawn $187,892 via wire transfer to the Fuck You, Be Glad I Left You a Dollar Bank of Athens.

So the wedding ring was off the list. I had removed one of the six items that told me my life was in order and prepared for another day of battle against the onslaught of the grind. I lit a cigarette and sat naked on the edge of the bed out of the mirror's line of sight.

I ran through it again. Keys, wallet, cigarettes, cell phone, watch. It was concise and certainly simpler. I liked the rhythm and it had a nice ring to it.

The ring.

I remembered yesterday's most impressive accomplishment.

I'd been driving to Vegas from LA in a roller coaster mixture of elation and rage with the music loud and the cruise control set at a hundred. For the past hour, I'd been holding the wedding ring, occasionally turning it around in my fingers pondering the beauty and social significance of its simplicity. And it's seamless completeness. I was torn between hurling it out the window or selling it and using the proceeds for one hand of blackjack. A winning hand would be an omen of better times ahead, but a loss would only reinforce my latest financial debacle. The last thing I needed was a reminder.

Thirty miles past Barstow, I passed a dead skunk on the side of the highway. After a quick U-turn, the overpowering stench left me wondering how long a skunk, like my defunct marriage, had to be dead before the smell disappeared. The body, while not decomposing, was in definite stages of decay. I knelt along the side of the road, oblivious to the speeding cars. Whatever questions the drivers may have had about the man dressed in shorts and a Hawaiian shirt kneeling alongside a dead skunk were of no concern to me.

It wasn't very big and, beneath its fur, the skunk looked skinny. I wondered if this was normal or if the skunk just hadn't eaten in a while. Its fur flickered as the desert wind gusted. The skunk was on its back, the body rigid with its legs stuck straight up in the air. The feet – or were they called paws – were perfectly symmetrical. Flip him over and he would make a perfect, yet unusual, little table. But where would you put it? Perhaps the zoo? A little zoo table. A place for all the resident skunks that didn't have to worry about getting whacked by speeding cars to rest their feet.

The only sign of bodily damage, apart from it being stiff as a board, was a missing toenail. Clipped off by the wheel of a speeding truck? Broken as he rolled from the impact? Lost in a fight with Mrs. Skunk? I studied the skunk's eyes. What do the eyes say about the last thing in any creature's mind the second before death? I recoiled from my own question. It was at that moment the voice returned.

Don't go there.

I cocked my head and waited. "Are you back?"

We'll see.

I nodded and refocused on the skunk. Its eyes portrayed shock. Shock from the impact, or maybe it had had time to ponder its impending fate. Few outward signs of damage, but an internal system scrambled and rearranged, the ability to function forever lost. I took the wedding ring from my shirt pocket and placed it on the skunk's left paw on the claw most resembling a ring finger.

I stood and stared down at the rigid body. The skunk appeared different. It was now a member of society's most sought after and misunderstood club. It had acquired the means to generate sympathy from passersby who might wonder if the skunk had kids and how the family must be devastated by the loss.

I decided it was time for a drink.

The skunk was dead. But I, although very much alone, was still alive. And I'd stumbled onto the perfect resting place for the ring. Thirty miles outside of Barstow, adorning a dead skunk's foot. Its life, like mine, permanently altered in the amount of time it takes to step in front of a speeding car.

Or out of the shower.

The pounding in my head was relentless and I knew from experience this would be an all-day hangover. I pulled on a bathrobe, sat on the edge of the bed and tried to summon details from last night. I came up blank.

That can't be good news.

I appreciated the voice's whisper. The more I tried to concentrate, the more my head pounded. My stomach churned and I tried to remember if I'd eaten dinner. A soft constant sound worked its way into my consciousness. Air conditioning? No. Running water.

I carefully hoisted myself off the bed and shuffled to the bathroom door and inched it open. Amidst the steam, I admired the muscular back of a woman washing her hair. I focused on the woman's taut buttocks. I continued the journey down her lean thighs and calves. My eyes drifted back to her tight bottom.

"World class," I whispered.

Despite the headache and nausea, I began to get aroused and cursed my alcohol consumption. To have shared intimacy with this woman would have been extraordinary. To not remember would be criminal. I silently pulled the door shut and returned to the edge of the bed. The water stopped, the sound replaced by familiar sounds of post-shower activity.

Who is she and how did she get up here?

I was hoping you'd be able to tell me.

A hooker, I decided. Given my condition last night, I couldn't imagine any other woman agreeing to a sleepover. The bathroom door opened and she appeared wearing a towel around her waist and another wrapped around her head. She jumped when she saw me.

"Sweet Jesus," she said, catching her breath. "You're up. I was going to leave you a note. Good morning." She cocked her head at me. "You look like shit."

A smile was fixed on her face as she watched me glance back and forth between her eyes and breasts. Making no attempt to cover herself, she stood still and allowed me some time. I marveled at their slight upward turn. The air conditioning applied the finishing touches.

They're perfect.

I nodded.

"Do you mind if I use one of your bathrobes?"

"As long as you don't mind if I ask you who you are and why you're in my room."

She laughed and padded softly across the carpet. She grabbed a bathrobe from the closet. She smiled and released the towel from around her waist.

"I'm Grace."

"Grace. As in state of?"

"That depends." She focused on untying the knot on the bathrobe's belt. "I'm here because you asked me. Besides, I wanted to make sure you got home safe."

I tried to focus on her words but was distracted by the sight of her sliding effortlessly into the plush robe. A knock on the door broke what was left of my concentration.

"Oh, good. Breakfast is here." She tightened the robe and went to the door. "Good morning, Ernesto. Just put everything on the table over there."

"Good morning, Grace. How was your evening?"

"Tragically uneventful."

The waiter chuckled as he rolled a large cart across the room. He noticed me sitting on the edge of the bed.

"Good morning, sir." His tone was cheerful and upbeat. I barely managed a nod in response.

"Thank you, Ernesto."

"My pleasure, Grace. Enjoy your breakfast."

He waved goodbye to her, smiled at me and departed. I continued to sit lifeless on the edge of the bed.

"Why don't you grab a quick shower before we eat?"

I looked at the woman who had taken charge and nodded. I stood and shuffled toward the bathroom.

"I'll get this set up. How do you like your coffee?"

From the bathroom doorway, I turned. "In solitude?"

She smiled and waited.

"Just cream," I said, closing the door behind me.

When I returned several minutes later she was fully dressed in a beautiful red evening gown. A memory returned. Green eyes. Red dress. I remembered first seeing her in one of the cocktail lounges late yesterday afternoon.

The shower helped. Now I sought additional assistance. She poured coffee and juice for both of us and started to eat. I watched the precise strokes she made with her knife and fork as I took a sip of juice and found it lacking. The coffee was more satisfying so I stayed with that. I warily eyed my breakfast. The woman called Grace noticed and reached into her purse. I accepted a small handful of aspirin and washed them down with a sip of juice.

"Thanks."

The woman finished chewing a mouthful of bagel and pointed at me with her fork. "You really shouldn't drink and gamble," she said, sipping her orange juice.

"By themselves, they're fine. But not in combination."

"That was my point." She continued to smile and study my face.

"How long were you with me at the tables last night?"

"Long enough."

My curiosity took over. "I lost…didn't I?" I caught a touch of sympathy in her expression. "How much?"

"About a hundred and fifty."

"We are talking thousands, right?"

She nodded and went to work on her omelet.

"Expensive day," I said.

330 thousand? Nice to meet you, Mr. Rockefeller.

The woman, oblivious to the voice, nodded in agreement. She finished her breakfast in silence as I went back and forth between watching her and staring down at my plate. I picked at my food but did manage to keep down three cups of coffee. The woman pushed her plate away and I lit a cigarette. She frowned, but said nothing. I coughed and sipped my juice.

"Look…Grace. Do I owe you any money?"

Her eyes flared briefly, but then relaxed. "Of course not. I'm not a hooker." She then turned playful. "But we should try this again when you're…"

"Sober?"

"I was going to say functional…but yeah, let's go with sober."

"I'm sober now." I forced a weak smile and shook my head. "Maybe not."

She laughed. "That's okay. It can wait. I'll be around."

"You live here in Vegas?"

"I work for the Casino."

Midway through a piece of bacon, I paused. "Doing what? I thought the idea of casino employees dating guests was a no-no."

"We're dating? How sweet." She laughed.

"What would you call it?"

"Oh, just keeping an eye out for someone who'd had way too much to drink."

She said it far too casually and, despite his hangover, my instincts kicked in. "So last night, did we…?"

"What do you think?"

"I'm betting my plumbing was out of order last night."

"Finally, you win a bet." She laughed at her joke and cocked her head. "You're staring. What?"

"I'm just wondering what your job is. You're so beautiful."

"You're too kind. Let's call it Guest Relations and leave it at that." She looked at her watch. "I need to run. And I definitely need to change. A woman wearing formal attire at six in the morning can only mean one thing." She stood and kissed him hard. "I'll see you soon."

I watched her leave and stared at the closed door, then crawled back into bed and dreamt hard.

Fortunately, the voice slept soundly.

* 9 7 8 1 9 4 2 6 9 1 0 1 3 *